THE HANDBOOK ON 47 PURE BREED DOGS WITH HERO DOG AWARDS BY EXCELLENT AND OUTSTANDING TRAINERS BETWEEN FROM 2000-2025

DR. HERBERT K. NAITO

To order additional copies of this book, contact:

Media Literary Excellence LLC

508 West 26th Street KEARNEY, NE 68848

402-819-3224

info@medialiteraryexcellence.com

TABLE OF CONTENTS

CHAPTER 1
Introduction

While all dog species love spending time with their owners, certain breeds relish being around people more than others, including the English Setters, Cocker Spaniels, and Smooth Collies. Dogs have long been known as a man's best friend, due to the love and companionship that they provide their owners that a spokesperson from The Kennel Club. The signs of a friendly dog breed include raised ears, a constantly waggling tail, and a willingness to approach humans without the signs of aggression. Some further characteristics found in friendly dog breeds include:

- ✓ A calm temperament
- ✓ Enjoys being in social situations
- ✓ Loves human companionship
- ✓ Like to play with other dogs and their owners
- ✓ Easy to train
- ✓ They are less likely to get anxious or fearful

If you are thinking of adopting a dog of your own, remember: a dog's behavior and temperament always depend on its training, socialization, and individual personality. Equally, regardless of a dog's personality, they must always be allowed enough space, peace, and quiet to rest. America has about *63.4 million* dogs and the world has *900 million* dogs! Approximately **39%** of the Americans own dogs! But I was presented with the Appreciation Award for the Hero Dog Award!

I asked the experts at The Kennel Club to recommend the friendliest breeds, the best known for loving adults and children and adolescents. Take a look at the dogs below:

Cocker Spaniel:

This breed of dogs is so synonymous with having a friendly nature that they are even known as the "Merry Cocker" An active and adventurous breed, with an ever-waggling tail, they love to shower their owners with affection and devotion, says a spokesperson from The Kennel Club. This breed has remained a family favorite since the early 20th century, due to their gentle and cheerful nature. This breed makes one of the best companions.

YOU'LL FIND ME

Figure 1: Cocker Spaniel (Adult): These dogs are friendly and will always connect with other dogs in the house and they are 2000 Hero Dog Award that will help the dog to become friendly with children and adolescents.

The Bichons are playful, friendly dogs who get on well with children, teens, and adults and entire family members. The species is a small dog with a happy and lively personality. They are fantastic family companions who love to show affection to their owners and enjoy spending days by their human's side. Related best dogs for families are English Setters.

English Setters:

As well as being very active, the English Setters are also known to be outgoing and a good-natured dog. Sadly, despite their lovable character, they have seen their population numbers decline, placing them on The Kennel Club's Vulnerable Native breed list! The list is that they love affection, they are a large breed so require an owner that can provide them with a lot of exercise and a large home and garden.

Figure 2: English Setters (Adult) are very loving dogs with Hero Dog Award during 2000.

This dog is a small breed from the Terrier family, characterized by its wiry coat and lively, affectionate personality. The previously owned by the Queen's uncle, HRH, The Duke of Gloucester, they are a typical terrier; but alert, extroverted and eager to please. The Australian Terrier is a welcoming breed suitable as a companion dog. This small dog breeds make the best companions.

Havanese:

This dog is known to be a lively, affectionate, and intelligent breed according to an expert from The Kennel Club. This dog loves to be with its owners, so if you can take this dog to work or you are at home for most of the day, a dog like this could be the breed that you will like.

Figure 3: Havanese (Adult) is a great dog for being friendly and received the Hero Dog Award during 2001.

Smooth Collie:

This dog is also known for their friendly and outgoing nature and is a strong and intelligent dog, originally bred to manage sheep, and still enjoy spending time outside.

They are a sociable and energetic breed also need to be active, and like outdoorsy owners. The smooth Collie is another breed that sadly classed as a vulnerable native breed, despite their endearing nature. This breed of dog also is agile and active dogs that excel in canine sports like agility. They tend to have seemingly endless energy that they love to burn out on long walks.

Figure 4: Smooth Collie (Adult) is a very active sport dog and received their Hero Dog Award during 2022.

German Shepard:

Height: 24-26 inches (Male)
       22-24 inches (Female)
Weight: 65-90 pounds (Male)
       50-70 pounds (Female)
Life Expectancy: 12-14 years

The German Shepherd dogs are one of the most popular breeds in the world, treasured for their intelligence, loyalty, and athleticism. They're large brown-and black dogs with a streamlined building that makes them both strong and agile. Though they're excellent herding dogs, and also very well suited to work as *service animals* such as guide dogs for the visually impaired. They also serve as police officers, members of the military, guard dogs, and even movie stars. They're undoubtedly versatile dogs; but they need owners who can give them enough ways to expand their energy and smarts. If you think that you can keep up, read on to learn more about the German Shepherd dog. This breed of dog are productive, loyal companions and they are bred with a strong work ethic, they are among the most popular dog breeds in the United States-number 4 in 2022-thanks in large part of their ability to be great family dogs. They love their people; but can be cautious around strangers or newcomers and thrive on the care and attention of their family.

Figure 5: German Shepherd (Adult male) is a very popular dog that received the Hero Dog Award during 2025.

Figure 6: German Shepherd (Adult female) is a very popular dog that received the Hero Dog Award during 2023.

Does your dog have some bad behaviors that they need to help getting rid of barks? As much as we love them, they aren't always perfect and it's extremely important that they get trained properly. One woman whose brother passed away had to find a home for his dog or he'd get sent to the animal pound. The problem was he just had the worst behavior problems imaginable, and she didn't know what to do! A person's story about barking was cute. The dog may hate their mailman; but their barking can be out of control! You can take your barking dog to a dog trainer, and it will cost $2,000 to stop the barking. Whenever your dog is performing badly, in your case, the barking at the door; then you would get in between him and the door and press the button on the Barks no more! The barks no longer are the fastest and most cost-efficient way to get rid of your pet's is poorly behave! The following dogs also need barking training.

Figure 7: Chihuahua is a tiny dog that can make a lot of problems by barking a lot or can make a lot of happiness to the owner and receive the Hero Dog Award.

Figure 8: Labrador Receiver is a magnificent dog and received the 2024 Hero Dog Award for the dog's attacking criminals at a bank.

Figure 9: Yuki-Poo is a tiny dog that attacked a child with poor behavior and received the Hero Dog Award during 2000.

Figure 9: Yuki-Poo is a tiny dog that attacked a child with poor behavior and received the Hero Dog Award during 2000.

Figure 10: German Shepherds with the 2025 Hero Dog Award were given because of their duty to stop the drug criminals.

Figure 11: Boxer was awarded the 2004 Hero Dog Award for stopping crooks attacking a food and alcohol store.

Figure 12: Husky was given the Hero Dog Award for stopping an adult male that was raping a child during 2025.

Figure 13: Winner Dog or Dachshund with a 2022 Hero Dog Award for chasing another dog for attacking a high school student that stole some ammunition from a gun store.

Figure 14: Bulldog that stopped a child from taking candy from a neighbor's house and the dog received the Hero Dog Award at 2001.

YOU'LL FIND ME

IN THE FOREST

Figure 15: Rottweilers are great dogs that are similar to the German Shepherds that are skillful for finding marijuana in secret places and obtained the Hero Dog Award in 2003.

Figure 16: Great Dane is a 2000 Hero Dog Award for protecting the owner's problems with their neighbor's temperament problems.

Figure 17: Poodle is a 2001 Hero Dog Award that has the personality to provide lots of kisses to a child that requires therapy heal their mental health sickness.

Figure 18: Yorkshire is a playful dog with children and received the Hero Dog Award in 2004.

Figure 19: Golden Retriever is a happy dog with the 2000 Hero Dog Award that provides a lot of affection to their family.

12

Figure 20: Labrador Receiver: is a huge dog with the 2001 Hero Dog Award to play with their family's other dog with a lot of pleasure.

This strain of dog is originally from Canada. More precisely, from a province located at the extreme East of the country bearing the same name-Labrador. In the XIXth century, the native Americans used them as water dogs and hunting dogs. However, the British are the ones who imposed the breed's characteristics in 1903, setting the scene for the Labrador Retriever that we now know.

Why are the labrador retrievers such a versatile dog breed? These dogs come with no surprises that they are fantastic family dogs! Instead, they are affectionate and cheerful. They have numerous assets, but the ones that stand out are their good character-love for their family and children. They have numerous assets; but the ones that stand out are their good character, love for.

Figure 23: Boxer (Adult) that the owners said that they are truly wonderful dogs that received the Hero Dog Award in 2025 because of their helpful intelligence.

The Boxers are truly wonderful dogs that are sassily trainable! Fortunately, utilizing a system of training which dogs readily understand, and which is neither compulsory nor reliant on food and bribes, the instructor's method is ideal for this working breed. The Boxer dog is absolutely dependent upon the companionship of their families! This is not a dog to be left alone unattended for hours on end. Boxer dogs are known for being loyal, intelligent, and high-energy. They are also known for being playful, loving, and protective. Boxer dogs from their fascinating origins to the best care practices. So, whether you're considering adding a Boxer to your family or you're already a proud Boxer parent, stick around for some insightful and engaging information.

The Boxer dog breed originated in Germany in the 19th century. These energetic and intelligent dogs were developed by crossing the now-extinct Bullenbeisser with mastiff-type dogs and bulldogs. The aim was to create a versatile working dog with strength, agility, and playful nature, making these Boxers well-suited for various roles from hunting to guarding people and their home. The Boxers have since been celebrated as excellent companions, therapy dogs, and even police dogs, thanks to their high energy and protective instincts. Whether as playful pets or diligent working dogs, Boxers have a unique place in the canine world!

Husky:

The Siberian Huskies are known for their high energy and athleticism, making them ideal companions for active individuals or families. Their thick coats may require a bit of extra grooming, but the work is worth it to snuggle up to these fluffy bundles of love. These dogs thrive on human interaction and make fantastic family pets. However, they have a bit of a mischievous streak and benefit from lots of exercise and enrichment. Siberian Huskies were originally bred by the Chukchi people of Northeastern Asia to help with transportation, hunting, and as companions. They were eventually brought to Alaska in the early 1900s to help with sled dog racing, and their popularity quickly spread from there. The Siberian Huskies are a beloved family pets and are often used for search-and-rescue missions due to their incredible endurance and strength.

How often should Huskies be groomed? Huskies should be brushed weekly with a rake brush that gently removes the old coat. If you create a routine of brushing your Husky's coat. If you create a routine of brushing your Husky once a week -and once a day during shedding seasons-then the problem can be mitigated. Additionally, when Huskies are not brushed regularly, this can lead to a buildup-oil and dander on their skin, causing irritation. Through Huskies are super shedders, their coats are actually self-cleaning. They do not require routine baths; you can bathe your Husky when needed but use a high-quality shampoo that will preserve the oils and color of their coat.

Can Huskies live in hot weather? Yes, Siberian Huskies can adapt to and live-in hot weather with proper care and precautions. They should be provided with plenty of cool shaded areas and lots of fresh water. Exercise should be limited to the coolest part of the day to prevent overheating. Make use of cooling mats, kiddie pools, and other tools like air-conditioning in the home. This should be part of the car if the dog is in the back seat.

Figure 24: Husky is a dog that loves riding an automobile during the winter rather than walking on the snow and received the Hero Dog Award during 2025.

Are Huskies healthy dogs? Yes, they are good family dogs. They are affectionate, gregarious, and friendly with everyone (And so do not make the ideal watchdog if that's what you're looking for). They are an extremely active breed, so an active family that enjoys the outdoor hiking and cold weather outdoor activities will make the best match for this breed. They are not well-suited to tropical climes, so they do best with the families who live in colder climates. It should also be noted that they can't be trusted off-leash as they love to ruan, so that they must always be kept on-leash when outdoors.

Husky health: and how often should Huskies be groomed? Huskies should be brushed weekly with a rake brush that gently removes old hair.

Dachshund:

Dachshunds, also known as Doxies, winner dog, sausage dog and are small, lively dogs with long bodies, short legs, and deep chests. The German work "Dachshund" translates to "badger dog" as they were originally bred in 18th century Germany to hunt badgers in their burrows. They come in two sizes: Standard and miniature, and three coat types; smooth, wirehaired, and longhaired. Dachshund dog breed of hound and terrier ancestry developed in Germany to pursue badgers into their burrows. The Dachshund is a long-bodied, characteristically lively dog with a long-bodied, characteristically lively dog with a deep chest, short legs, tapering muzzle, and long ears. Usually reddish brown or black-and-tan, it is bred in two sizes: standard and miniature and three coat types: smooth, longhaired, and wirehaired. The standard Dachshund stands about 8 to 9 inches tall at the withers and weighs 16 to 32 pounds. The miniature is shorter and weighs no more than 11 pounds. The dachshund requires a chance to run, sniff, and investigate daily, preferably in a fenced yard supplemented with lash walks. A miniature longhair variety is perhaps better suited for apartment living-but other miniature varieties might also do well in that environment because of its independent nature and tendency to follow scent trails, a Dachshund should not be let off the leash in unfenced areas. Dachshunds enjoy a variety of games, including chasing balls. They especially love sports that test a dog's hunting abilities, such as the barn hunt. In addition, many enjoy racing events as "wiener dog" competitions. Their coat cares for the smooth variety requires only occasional brushing to remove dead hair. The long back, short legs, and big chest are typical of this dog.

The physical characteristics include:

❖ **Size:** Miniature dachshunds are usually 15-20 cm tall and weigh 4-5 kg.
❖ **Coat:** They can have smooth, long, or wire hair.
❖ **Colors:** They can be chocolate, tan, blue, black and tan, red, cream, dapple, sable, piebald, brindle, and wild boar.
❖ **Eyes:** They have almond-shaped eyes that can be dark red or black and brown.

Figure 25: Dachshund are very playful dogs, but are motivated to be calm and sociable with the children and adolescents and received the Hero Dog Award in 2023.

Temperament:

- ❖ Dachshund temperaments are bright, loyal, and courageous. These little dogs have large barrel chests to give them stamina while hunting a trait that can also translate into lots of running around and barking.
- ❖ **Extraversion:** Refers to how energetic and outgoing a dog is.
- ❖ **Motivation:** Refers to how self-assured a dog is.
- ❖ **Training focus:** How responsive a dog is during training.
- ❖ **Amicability:** How friendly and sociable a dog is.
- ❖ **Neuroticism:** Reflects nervous sensitivity in a dog.
- ❖ **Personality types in dogs:** Is typically assessed using a variation of The Big Five personality assessment for humans. The research has identified similar personality dimensions in dogs which include:

1. **Extraversion:** Refers to how energetic and outgoing a dog is.
2. **Motivation:** Refers to how self-assured a dog is.
3. **Training Focus:** How responsive a dog is during training.
4. **Amicability:** How friendly and sociable a dog is.
5. **Neuroticism:** Reflects nervous sensitivity in a dog.

The most Dachshund is a calmest dog because the wire-haired dachshunds have terrier in their lineage, they're often less calm than their long-haired cousins, who are the quietist and calmest of the three types. Dachshunds with a smooth coat tend to have a personality that falls somewhere in the middle. Because the wire-haired Dachshunds have terrier in their lineage, they're often less calm than their long-haired cousins, who are the quietest and calmest of the three types. Dachshunds with a smooth coat tend to have a personality that falls somewhere in the middle. The dog is playful, feisty, stubborn, fond of cuddling-that this little dog is a mixed bag. If trained well, Dachshunds can make excellent companions, steadfast family dogs, and even therapy dogs. If not, they can be overwhelming and a little difficult to control. Like with many dog breeds, it's good to remember their original purpose, which is to be a hunter's companion. All those qualities that can make a Dachshund exasperate are what also make the dog uniquely gifted.

> *6. Ideal pet parent for a Dachshund:* Who love apartment life because of their small size, they don't need a backyard, but they do enjoy going on walks outside. Dachshunds also love a challenge, and as long as you incorporate plenty of opportunities to chase and find things, you'll have a happy dog.

7. These dogs love their owners and really don't want them to leave: *Your* dog may struggle more with separation anxiety, and when they're missing you, they're likely to chew. When you do leave your home without your dog, you may want to use a kennel.

8. Training is key for this dog breed: Like many small dogs, these are prone to show aggression toward strangers and other dogs, and a loud bark that can make the process of training a bit more complicated. Families with small children should only get a Dachshund if they are committed to consistent training and regular socializing as they are more likely than other dogs to bite their owners and kids.

9. Why should you have these dogs? These dogs are intelligent, independent, and playful, but can also be mischievous and stubborn. They aren't the easiest breeds to housebreak or train. If you leave your home without the dog, you may want to use a kennel.

10. Dachshund grooming: These beloved dogs are low-maintenance pups that don't shed too much or need too many baths, but depending on their coat type (Smooth, wire hair, or long hair), they'll be different amounts of grooming needed. Long haired dogs need the most frequent grooming of all, while smooth Dachshunds only need a simple wipe down with a cloth between baths. Wire-haired Dachshunds will need regular brushing every two days, that should be enough, and twice per year, they'll need their coats stripped with a special brush.

11. Dog's health: Dachshunds are more likely to experience epilepsy, granulomatous meningoencephalitis, Cushing's Syndrome, thyroid and autoimmune issues, and various eye defects. Double dapple dogs are more prone to hearing and vision problems.

12. Back injuries: don't let the dog jump down from high spots, and keep their backs supported when you carry them. They're also susceptible to weight gain, which can put even more strain on their backs. Many owners opt for pet insurance plans.

Great Dane:

The Great Dane are also known as the German Mastiff, is a giant, powerful, and regal-looking dog breed. It is one of the Best-natured dogs around, the Great Dane is courageous and protective, with a steady, but sensitive temperament. Overall, these affectionate canines are a healthy breed, and despite their large size, prefer life indoors, close to their large size, prefer life indoors, close to their human companions. For those seeking both a protector and a cuddler with a low-key attitude, look no further than the majestic Great Dane.

The Great Danes are not from Denmark. They are modern dog ancestors that are the mastiff-type canines who served as hunting and war companions as far back as 3000 BCE. Several countries began refining traits of these early dogs through selective breeding, but it was Germany who organized the breed that we recognized today. In 1870, the country recognized its "Deutsche Dogge" as the national dog. By the mid-1800s, American breeders were importing the dogs from Germany, breeding them to improve the temperament and appearance of the breed.

When it comes to choosing a dog, finding one with a calm temperament and obedient nature can make all the difference-especially for those who value peaceful companionship. One of the overall affectionate canines are a healthy breed, and despite their large size, prefer life indoors, close to their owner and children. By the mid-1800s, American breeders were importing the dogs from Germany, breeding them to improve their elegant appearance, the Great Dane is a working breed. They do their best when they have a purpose, whether it's keeping watch over the family, playing games with their owners, or participating in agility or obedient activities. These gentle, low-key dogs often serve animals and can perform tasks for people with physical, emotional, psychiatric, intellectual, or sensory challenges due to their size, Great Danes also work as brace dogs for those who need assistance standing and walking.

1. *Great Danes are better inside dogs than outside dogs:* These amazing dogs aren't yard dogs. Great Danes prefer to be close to their owners indoors. They don't tolerate the cold very well and the owners should never leave them alone outdoors for long periods, especially in colder climates. Even though these huge dogs are clumsy as puppies, they adapt well to the smaller homes or apartments due to their laid-back temperament. The breed experts recommend crate training.

2. *The Great Danes are Big:* They can grow to a height of 28 to 32 inches at the shoulder. The males generally weigh between 140 and 175 pounds when fully grown.

The females are a bit smaller, reaching an adult weight of 110 to 140 pounds. Yet, these gentle canines seem oblivious to their size and see themselves as lap dogs. Dane puppies grow fast. The owners are often shocked to see that their Dane puppy has grown visibly bigger overnight. They don't reach physical maturity until around the age of three.

3. The Great Danes are super-sensitive dogs: While some large breeds require a firm hand, the Great Danes do not. They don't respond to hard correction or training methods. Many breeders say that gentler speech and mannerisms work best. The Great Danes need socialization from the age of three months to six months, then obedience training with praise and rewards should begin because this breed has an innate desire to please, training helps them learn acceptable behavior and leads to a happier, more confident pet. Their instinct is to be friendly, courageous, and never timid.

4. Great Danes are excellent family dogs: People seeking a watchdog that they can also trust around children should consider a Great Dane. Protective, yet not overly aggressive, Great Danes are naturally intimidating due to their loud bark and large size. However, if these dogs feel threatened or feel that their human family is in danger, they will exhibit aggressive behavior towards the threat. Otherwise, they know how to be gentler around children. Their high affection levels and sweet, playful nature make them an excellent family dog.

5. Great Danes has a variety of coat colors: The American Kennel Club recognizes nine different Great Dane coat colors-black, fawn, black and white, are among those listed as official standards for registered dogs. However, there are several other variations of these coats as well available from the professional breeders. Great Danes may also wear a black mask. In the past, breeders practiced a cosmetic procedure called cropping on puppies' ears before selling them. The practice is controversial among owners around the world. Natural-eared Danes are now becoming the norm.

6. Great Danes have specific inherited health concerns: Most dog breeds have specific inherited conditions that could appear during your pet's lifetime. Although a generally healthy, robust dog, some Great Danes are predisposed to inherited diseases:

❖ Congenital heart defects and cardiomyopathy and regular veterinarian exams and echocardiograms are recommended.
❖ Hip dysplasia: Orthopedic Foundation for Animals certifications means that the parents have undergone examination and found to be free of hip dysplasia. Penn Hip testing shows the risk of your puppy developing hip dysplasia.

❖ Bloat: Number one killer of Great Danes. Multiple small meals and no vigorous exercise immediately before or after mealtimes help prevent it.
❖ Wobblers Syndrome: A neurological disease that affects the spine in adolescent Danes and can be congenital or trauma induced.

7. *Great Danes eat* a *lot.* A proper diet is essential for these giant dogs. Adult Danes eat around 10 cups of food per day, split into two or more meals each day. If they eat too much or eat too fast, they risk bloat, a serious stomach torsion issue that traps gas and cuts off the blood supply. As puppies feeding Great Danes a dog food that is specifically for large breeds that will provide the right amount of protein and prevent your dog from growing too fast and damaging bones and joints. It's a good idea to speak with your veterinarian about your pet's habits:

Figure 26: Great Dane (Adult) grow fast to be large and run very fast to catch a person in the family and received the Hero Dog Award I 2020.

✓ *Large appetite*: Their large stature requires a substantial number of calories to maintain.
✓ *Puppy stage*: Great Dane puppies eat even more proportionally during their growth spurt.
✓ *Proper diet.* It's important to feed them high-quality large-breed dog food designed to support their joint health.
✓ *Consult* a *vet.* Always consult your veterinarian to determine the appropriate amount of food for your individual Great Dane based on their weight and activity level. The dog will eat about 4 cups of Purina dry food.
✓ *Despite their glossy coat and elegant appearance, the great Dane* is a *working breed.* They do their best when they have a purpose, whether it's keeping watch over the family, playing games with their owner, or participating in agility or

21

obedience activities. These gentle, low-key dogs often serve animals and can perform tasks for people with physical, emotional, psychiatric, intellectual, or sensory challenges. Due to their size, Great Danes also work as brace dogs for those who need assistance standing and walking.

✓ *Great Danes are super-sensitive dogs:* While some large breeds require a firm hand, Great Danes do not! They don't respond to hard correction or training methods. Many breeders say that gentler speech and mannerisms work best. Because this breed

✓ *Great Danes are super-sensitive dogs:* While some large breeds require a firm hand, Great Danes do not! They don't respond to hard correction or training methods. Many breeders say that gentler speech and mannerisms work best. Because this breed has an innate desire to please, training helps them learn acceptable behavior and leads to a happier; more confident pet. Their instinct is to be friendly, courageous, and never timid.

✓ *Great Danes are excellent family dogs:* Great Danes are naturally intimidating due to their lard bark and large size! However, if these dogs feel threatened or feel that their human family is in danger; they will exhibit aggressive behavior towards the threat. Otherwise, they know how to be gentler around children. Their high affection levels and sweet, playful nature make them an excellent family dog!

✓ *Great Danes can be a violent dog with nasty kids:* When they attack small children, they will bite the kid's face and throat! Or head and neck. The owner of the dog should train them properly, so they don't attack children, teens, and adults. There are many other breeds of dogs that can attack children with the same type of behaviors of pit bulls, bull dogs, or by German Shepherds.

✓ *According to the American Academy of Pediatrics,* children and adults with dog bites should receive a tetanus shot, or booster tetanus vaccine or receive one within the last 5 years. You may need two rabies vaccine (3 days apart) and rabies immunoglobulin (HRIG] as well as tetanus shot. The dog bits should also be washed with soap and water. You may need medicine to fight dog bites immediately and don't get any infections!

- ❖ Average height: 14-24 inches.
- ❖ Average weight: 45-75 pounds.
- ❖ Average lifespan: 10-16 years.

Do they shed Standard Poodles: They are low-shedding breed, making them a good choice for people with allergies or those who prefer less hair around the house. They are often considered hypoallergenic, however, it's essential to note that no dog is truly hypoallergenic. Regular grooming and brushing can help minimize *shedding.*

How big do *Standard Poodles* get? They have a well-proportional body with a straight, strong back, and a long, graceful neck. Their head is refined with a straight muzzle, almond-shaped eyes, and floppy ears that hang close to the head. Their coat is dense and curly and can come in various solid colors such as black, white, apricot, and more colors.

When do Standard Poodles stop growing? Most Standard Poodles reach their full height by the time that they're around 12 to 15 months old. However, they may continue to fill out and develop muscle until they're about two years old.

What is a *royal Standard Poodle?* There isn't an official or recognized breed called "royal Standard Poodle." The term "royal" is often used informally to describe larger-than-average Standard Poodles who exceed the usual size for the breed, often standing taller and weighing more than the standard height and weight guidelines.

Health problems of Standard Poodles: They have hypoallergenic dogs because they produce less dander and shed less compared to many other breeds. However, no dog is completely hypoallergenic. People with allergies may still react fit for allergies.

How much exercise does a Standard Poodle need? They are moderately active dogs that benefit from daily exercises to stay healthy and happy. A combination of daily walks, playtime, and mental stimulation is usually sufficient to meet their exercise needs. Aim for at least 30 to 60 minutes of physical activity per day, but keep in mind the owner.

Are Standard Poodles prone to cancer? Unfortunately, Standard Poodles are among the breeds that are known to have a higher predisposition to contain types of cancer, Hemangiosarcoma, must cell tumors, and transitional cell carcinoma are some of the cancers that can affect these dogs. While genetics can play a role, a healthy lifestyle and seeing a vet will be important! There are three main types of poodles:

❖ *Standard Poodle*: This dog has been adequately described above with a lot of details.
❖ *Miniature poodle*: a descendant of the Standard Poodle, standing 10-15 inches at the shoulder and weighing 15-17 pounds.

❖ Toy poodle: This is the smallest type of poodle, standing 10 inches or less at the shoulder and weighing 6-9 pounds.

This breed is divided into 4 varieties based on their size, the Standard Poodle, medium poodle, Medium Poodle, Miniature poodle, toy poodle all shares the same breed standard, which is a fancy way of saying that they all look alike. Their heights and weights are proportionate, and they all can be groomed in the same fanciful ways. In fact, when you think of the Poodle's appearance, you possibly think of the Poodle's appearance, you probably think of the big poufy pompadour and snowball-shaped socks. And look:

1. *Ears*: Poodle ears are long, set at or below eye level and hang down.

2. *Eyes*: Their eyes are dark and oval.

3. *Nose*: They have long and pointed noses.

4. *Coat length*: The poodle dog's coat is curly, dense, and often clipped short.

5. *Coat Color*: Poodle colors can be a range of colors, including black, brown, apricot, cream, café au lait, blue, red, silver, silver beige, grey, or white. Their color is even and solid throughout the body.

6. **Tail:** Their tails are naturally long and straight. The AKC breed standard calls for the tail to be docked. Docking involves cutting a portion of the dog's tail off when they are puppies. Veterinary groups along with many U.S. states and countries have banned this procedure due to medical and behavioral reasons. If you are interested in this procedure, schedule a consultation with your veterinarian.

7. *Poodle temperament*: They have been typecast as prissy, silly or neurotic, but in reality, this active dog breed defies Hollywood stereotypes with their outgoing, friendly and eager-to-please personality. However, their temperament can be influenced by the mood of those around them like poodles who live in chaotic households or homes where people are barely home may resort to attention-seeking behavior, such as barking or chewing. That's because Poodles form deep, loving bonds with their pet parents and prefer to spend time with you over almost anything else. That's not to say that they can't be alone:

• Their innate intelligence enables them to excel in obedience and earl y socialization, so if you properly train them to be comfortable with being alone, they'll be fine.

- There are always exceptions to any rule, but generally Poodles are ge nerally Poodles that are a high-anxiety breed.

How to care for a poodle:

You think that a poodle's a delicate flower? Hardly a breed as hunting dogs with superior running and swimming skills. Poodles are a hardy breed group who love to show off. They'll absorb new knowledge their whole lifelong and are always up for training such new tricks. They adore spending time out-doors socializing with people and pets and of course, going on adventures with their BFF:

Grooming: The poodles are distinctive, curly coat is frequently groomed in one of three spectacular ways:

English Saddle: The dog is shaved all over, except for puffs on the head, bottom of the legs and the top of the tail.

Continental: The traditional "French Poodle" cut.

Sporting clip: The face, feet, neck, and base of the tail are shaved, but a pouf is left on the head and tail while the rest of the body is cut to 1 inch, like a short blanket.

You *don't have* to *groom:* A Poodle like they're headed to the show ring, though. Many pet parents opt to let their dogs go au *naturel.*

Let's clear up some misconceptions: About their trademark froufrou coat. That distinctive cut-the furry "bracelets" on their ankles, followed by closely shaved legs known as the Continental clip-has a working dog background. Historically, people groomed Poodles that way to maximize their waterfowl-hunting abilities. The fur around their joints kept them warm I cold water, while the rest of their closely shaven body would reduce drag while chasing after ducks. Today, fancy Poodle styles are mostly for aesthetics. How you style your dog is completely up to you! Just be sure to follow these basic grooming tips:

- For routine grooming, you'll need a slicker brush to brush your pup every day; be sure to get all the way to the skin to prevent mats. The more thoroughly you brush your Poodle, the less frequently you have to bathe them.
- You should bathe your Poodle every 4 to 8 weeks unless they have a mud bath. You can find a dog's shampoo formulated specifically for Poodles, which can boost the color of light or white-colored poodles. Their fur will dry quickly

(Remember that they're a water-loving breed) or you can use a high-velocity dryer designed for dogs.

➤ Check their eyes for tear stains. Tear stains are streaks that discolor your pup's fur. This eye discharge is your pup's fur. This eye discharge is your pup's way of getting rid of debris in the eye. Even though the tears are clear, there's a pigment in the tears that stains your dog's hair. Use a damp washcloth or eye care wipes to gently clean the fur around your pup's eyes.

➤ Your Poodle's cute and floppy ears also need some TLC. Check their ears at least once a week, looking for buildup, hair growth or bad odors. You may need to pluck or trim the hair in their ears with rounded shears. Ask your vet at your puppy's first well visit what to watch for and how best to clean their ears.

➤ Your pup will need a haircut every four to eight seeks, right alongside bath time.

➤ If you take your pup to a groomer, ask them to trim your dog's nails. If you hear their nails clicking on the hardwood floor, though, you may hear their nails clicking on the hardwood floor, though, you may need to give your pup a pedicure in between spa dates.

➤ Be sure to brush your pup's teeth daily. Have your vet show you how if you need help. Start brushing those pearly whites while your dog's a puppy since Poodles are prone to periodontal disease, and have your vet professionally clean their teeth once a year for optimal dental health.

➤ Poodles are a generally healthy dog breed. Like all dogs, they're prone to certain health conditions, but compared to most other breeds, they have fewer genetic health issues. Poodles have variable lifespans depending on their size. Though exceptions exist, toy, miniature and standard Poodles can live up to 18 years. However, there are some health issues to be aware of to help your Poodle have a happy, long life and also:

▪ *Hip Dysplasia*: Poodles may be susceptible to hip dysplasia, a condition in which the ball and socket of the hip joint don't fit together correctly, which can cause mobility issues. The hip dysplasia has a genetic and environmental component. The treatment is physical therapy, medication and surgery in severe cases.

▪ *Patellar Luxation*: This often-genetic orthopedic condition results when the kneecap is able to slip in and out of place resulting in potential lameness, pain, and arthritis. Treatment options include weight management, joint supplements pain medication and in severe cases will be surgery.

- *Hypothyroidism:* This disease occurs when thyroid doesn't produce enough thyroid hormone, which can lead to weight gain, lethargy, and hair loss. Hypothyroidism is typically easily detected with a simple blood test and treated with an oral prescription medication.
- **Eye** *Issue:* Some poodles may be susceptible to eye issues, including the following:

  1. Cataracts

  2. Optic nerve hypoplasia which you can be born with it.

  3. Progressive retinal atrophy

  4. Glaucoma

All 4 issues can cause blindness, but surgery can treat cataracts and glaucoma. The good news is that Poodles can live a happy life even if they lose their sight and can learn to rely on other senses.

- *Sebaceous adenitis:* This skin disease can inflame the sebaceous glands (Glands on the skin are responsible for lubricating the skin and hair follicles). This condition can lead to hair loss, scaly skin, or irritated patches on the dog's skin.
- *Mitral valve disease:* Poodles can be prone to a heart condition where the valves on the left side of the dog's heart leak. This usually is picked up by your vet as a heart mummer. If your vet hears a heart mummer, they will likely refer you to a veterinary cardiologist for an echocardiogram I A ultrasound of the heart) to determine the cause.
- *Addison's Disease:* This endocrine condition is often seen in Poodles occurs when the body does not make enough of its own natural steroid-cortisol. This can present as an acute emergency situation where the dog collapses or can be a more chronic presentation of weight loss, lethargy and vomiting and diarrhea. Your vet can perform blood tests to diagnose Addison's disease and start your pup on the necessary treatment plan. Preventative care is essential. Help your pup maintain a healthy weight; provide ample opportunities for exercise and brush their teeth. Also, note any time that your Poodle seems in pain or changes their behavior, such as losing interest in food or toys, or acting more lethargic or irritable than usual. If you see any of these changes, contact your vet.

> *There are 5 Poodle facts:*

1. These dogs were initially bred in Germany to be duck hunters. Then France downsized them to be toys.

2. They're an incredibly versatile breed. They hunt to do agility, nose work, barn hunt, and do Fast cat (A 100-yeard dash chasinga lure), confirmation and trucking.

3. In the mid-1970s, one Iditarod participant created a sled team partially made of Poodles, and the dogs put up a good race against more traditional sled dog breeds like Huskies.

4. Poodles can be clowns: joyous, friendly eager to please, and they love their families. They want to be with their owners.

5. Poodle coats shed very little, making the breed a popular choice if you have allergies or want a dog that doesn't require much vacuuming.

Figure 27. You should be looking for a charming dog with a lot of love for the owner's family members and is a member of the Hero Dog Award that was earned in 2004.

Yorkshire:

If you're looking for a whole lot of cute and charming dogs, the Yorkshire Terrier is a great option. These little balls of fluff are tiny in size. They are not your average dogs. They have unique needs and behaviors that require a different approach. So, they are NOT your average dog!

Most Yorkshire puppies start to calm down as they approach their maturity age, which is usually around 12 months, but for larger breeds it can be more likely to occur between 18 months and 2 years. The puppies' energy levels follow a rough timeline as they grow into adult dogs, from their first few weeks all the way through maturity, but you may find that they're at their most hyper at two stages in their journey. The first stage occurs between 10 to 16 weeks. It is also known as the teenage phase; this stage is where their rebellious streak kicks in. Don't be alarmed if they start acting up and ignoring your command of literally anything else in the room. It's important to persevere with basic dog training here and stop inappropriate dog chewing using lots of positive reinforcement.

A second wind of increased energy might come between 6 to 12months of age, and the puppies at this age can bring continued boundary testing and mischievous behaviors if they become bored. Continuing their training, socializing and play sessions during this stage that will help redirect that mischievous energy and keep your puppy's physically and mentally engaged.

Figure 28: Yorkshire (Yorkipoo) is a very friendly dog and received their Hero Dog Award in 2025.

When does a puppy become a dog?

If you've just welcomed your puppy home, then make the most of your little bundle of fluff, because before you know it they'll have doubled in size and you'll be heading out to buy a new collar! You also will need a 6-foot leash for your dog. Your Yorkshire will also need naps.

1. ***Create Structure***: The first, and maybe most useful while your puppy is so young, would be to create structure. By sticking to a routine and having specific time windows for things like feeding,

walks, toilet breaks outside, and play sessions. Your puppy will learn what to expect from their day. This reduces the risk of them becoming stressed and also helps to limit hyperactivity to certain times of the day (playtime).

2. *Create training.* You could also try creating training, which provides a safe space for your pup to settle and can help them differentiate between chill time and go time. As much as they might think they can run all day, your puppy needs regular naps and rest to ensure that they stay healthy and their bones develop correctly, so a create, or dedicated doggy den is perfect for this. Giving your pup a space that is just for them can also help with barking through the night.

3. *Meet their Exercise Needs.* You'll also want to make sure that your pup is getting the right amount of exercise for their age. Look for positive outlets that can channel their energy, whether that's a quick game of fetch or playing hide and seek in the house, practicing their obedience training or using interactive toys like a kong or snuffle mat. These outlets are great for reducing boredom. The brain games for dogs help to provide mental stimulation, which in turn can reduce mischievous behaviors.

4. *Walks and Socialization:* Another way to channel their energy is through walks and socialization, both of which stimulate a pup physically and mentally. If your pup is fully vaccinated, you'll be able to hit the streets, but if you're still waiting for their second vaccine to take your puppy for a walk, why not arrange a playdate in the garden or backyard with a friend or family member's vaccinated pup? You can catch up with a friend, while your pups engage in a little harmless wrestling! A few of my top tips for calming your hyper puppy:

✓ *Build a routine.* The structure will help eliminate boredom, inducing misbehaviors and may save a chair leg from being chewed!
✓ *Channel their energy through positive outlets:* While you're waiting for their vaccinations. A few play sessions with
✓ chewing toys or squeaky toys and hiding treats around the house are great places to start and will get their minds racing.
✓ *Enroll in a puppy training class:* Once your pup has had their last vaccine. With your help and that of a skilled dog trainer, they will safely learn the basics in obedience and also start to socialize with other pups of a similar age. Both of these factors can provide much needed mental development for the younger dogs.

✓ **Be patient:** I know that this may seem challenging at times, but the calmer you stay, the calmer that they will be! By getting stressed or angry with your puppy, you risk exacerbating the situation, which can cause more hyperactivity. So remember to breath, and approach puppyhood with an owner and positive approach. And finally, maybe the most important thing of all by remembering to have fun and find your inner puppy! Explore the world with your new best friend, heading to new places and maybe even building new friendships at the park, taking pleasure in the silliness that they bring to your life while you help them learn and grow. If you do all of this, there's no doubt that your energetic puppy will grow into a calm and loving companion when the parents reach the older dog years.

✓ **Golden Retrievers:** They were descended from the Labrador receivers from 1800s Newfoundland, the golden retrievers are a unique breed that has captured America's heart. Its subtype, the English cream golden retriever (Also called the white golden retriever), is loyal, trainable, intelligent, and gentle, making them perfect for any family. As part of the sporting family and gundog group, the white golden retrievers were initially bred to find or retrieve wounded games (Birds and rabbits) for their sport-hunting owners. Today, the English cream golden retrievers are described as intelligent and confident and, like English Labs, are less energetic than their American counterparts. Golden retrievers are famous for their easy-going disposition, gentle personality, and mellow moods. At Snowy Pines, people continue the white golden retriever's pure bloodline by breeding the healthiest dogs with the calmest and friendliest temperaments possible. Rated one of the nation's top breeders and trainers of white golden retrievers and white lab puppies. Snowy Pines continues to be the best option when searching for the perfect English cream golden retriever.

With them, you get the healthiest, happiest, best-behaved golden retriever and white lab puppies with the most potent bloodlines. So, if you want to add white golden retriever puppies to your home, start your journey today by browsing through Snowy Pines available puppies. The key to healthy and happy golden retriever puppies is parents that are treated the same. They select the most superior bloodlines and ensure an environment where their dogs can socialize and thrive for their whole lives. You can learn more about their puppy parents at Snowy Pines, and you'll see how easy it is to guarantee healthy puppies with the sweetest temperaments. When you choose Snowy White Labs, you get the happiest and healthiest English golden retriever puppies. If you're looking to add a loving English cream golden retriever to your family, then look no further, they are experienced, dedicated, trained, and ready to answer any questions that you may have.

If you're looking for a sweet, fluffy new pup with a gentle and loving disposition, you'll want to meet their white golden retriever puppies. They're excited to offer English cream golden retriever puppies for sale at Snowy Pines White Labs. You can meet the dams and sires that are currently producing a litter below. Head on over to their puppy lives stream to see some of these cuties in action! These are medium to large dogs that are typically 21 to 24 inches tall and weigh 55 to 75 pounds. The male Golden Retrievers are usually slightly larger than the females.

Figure 29: Golden Retriever (Adult) is an excellent and outstanding dog that received the Hero Dog Award for their proper attitude in 2002.

Their experience is more than just adding a puppy to the family and from health to training, to years of support that they pride themselves in being the best in USA! All their puppies are trained by their certified trainers and Snowy Pines is renowned as the best training program in the USA. All their puppies also have a personal training coach once they go home! At Snowy Pines the puppies cost $7500!

Pit Bull dog:

The decision to adopt a pit bull is filled with anticipation, love, and a dash uncertainty. With their muscular build and the reputation that precedes them, these dogs are a bundle of love, loyalty, and liveliness waiting to be unraveled. However, like with any breed, there are specific nuances that potential pit bull parents should be well-versed in and as you contemplate opening your home and heart to a pit bull, these insights aim to provide a well-rounded understanding, preparing you for a rewarding journey filled with love, loyalty, and the joy of having a loyal companion by your side.

❖ *Skin and Gastrointestinal Sensitivities:* Pit bulls *are* known for their robust physique, but beneath that tough exterior lies a sensitivity, especially when it comes to their skin and gastrointestinal health. A diet rich in high-quality, natural ingredients is paramount to keep their skin irritation-free and their digestive system functioning optimally. It's not merely about aesthetics or a shiny coat:

❖ It's about ensuring your pit bull leads a comfortable, itch-free life with a tummy that's at ease.

❖ *Dog intolerance*: Socialization isn't just a modern-day dog parenting buzzword:

❖ It's a crucial aspect of raising a well-adjusted pit bull.

❖ Right from puppyhood, your pit bull should be exposed to other dogs and various environments to foster a sense of security and friendliness curbing the inherent dog intolerance that can manifest if left unchecked.

❖ Regular playdates, dog park visits, and obedience classes are excellent avenues for socialization.

❖ Manage your pit bull's interactions with other dogs more effectively with the *Pet Safe Gentle Leader No-Pull Dog Headcollar.*

❖ *Separation Anxiety:* The pit bulls are incredibly family-oriented dogs. Their world revolves around their human pack, and separation from the family can trigger anxiety. A structured routine, interactive toys, and ensuring someone is around for the better part of the day that can help alleviate separation anxiety. It's about creating a secure environment where your pit bull feels loved and safe, even when you're not around.

❖ *Emotional well-being:* The emotional spectrum of pit bulls is vast. They are capable of a wide range of emotions, and a change in the household dynamics or routine can affect their emotional well-being. Consistency, love, and a peaceful environment contribute to a mentally healthy pit bull. They thrive on love and reassurance, and a stable, loving home is the bedrock of their emotional well-being. Support the emotional well-being of your pit bull with the *Shawn Co Essential Dog Harness.*

❖ *Misconception* of *"nanny dogs:"* The historical tag of "nanny dogs" often associate with pit bulls can be misleading while they can be gentle and loving with children, unsupervised interactions that are not advisable, especially with young children.

❖ *Puppy Care:* This is very important to implement to make the puppy warm and loving. A puppy is house trained, registered, and vet checked. It has all the health records and is ready to go today! They are very playful, love the company of kids, and other household pets like cats and other dogs.

Figure 30: Pit Bull (Adult) is an excellent dog that loves walking during the day as well as the evening and received I the Hero Dog Award in 2025.

Pit bull terriers can make excellent family pets when raised and trained responsibly. They are known for their loyalty, affection, and willingness to please their owners. However, like any dog breed, these dogs require early socialization, consistent training, and positive reinforcement to thrive in a family environment! When an owner was taking their dog for a walk one evening when a stupid adolescent person standing at a bus stop with who I presumed was his grandfather; did what you should never do to any dog, particularly one that's unfamiliar:

- ❖ He suddenly leaned into a person's face and yelled "woof. "The damned kid made me jump, never mind our dog. The person jumped back but didn't even bare their teeth. If they had reacted, that wretched brat could have lost half of his face and cost their life.
- ❖ Looking for ways to earn money online in addition to a person's part-time job, but you know how it is-the internet is full of scams and shady-Grady stuff, so a person spends weeks trying to find something legit!

What is ***Free cash all about?*** Basically, it's a platform that pays you for testing applications testing games or completing surveys. A person loves playing games, so completing surveys. This helps developers improve their applications while you make some money.

- ❖ You can earn by downloading applications, testing games or completing surveys. People love playing games, so that's where most of their earnings came from (Oh, and people's favorites were Warpath, Wild Fish, and Domino Dreams).

- ❖ There's a variety of offers (Usually, the higher-paying ones that take more time).
- ❖ Some games can pay up to $1,000 for completing a task, but these typically require more hours to finish.
- ❖ On average, you can easily earn $30-60 per day.
- ❖ You pick your options, you're free to choose whatever applications, games, and surveys that you like.

The emotional spectrum of pit bulls is vast. They are capable of a wide range of emotions, and a change in the household dynamics or routine can affect their emotional well-being. Consistency, love, and reassurance, and a stable, loving home is the bedrock of their emotional well-being. Support the emotional well-being of your pit bull with the *Shawn Co Essential Dog Harness.*

The historical tag of "nanny dogs" often associated with the dogs can be misleading while they can be gentle and loving with children and adolescents, unsupervised interactions that are not advisable, especially with very young children. Every dog, irrespective of the breed, has its tolerance threshold, and educating children on the right way to interact with dogs is essential.

The musical inclination of pit bulls is a lesser-known, whimsical facet of their personality. Some pit bulls exhibit a keen sense of music and rhythm. They might bark along to your favorite tunes, wag their tail to the beat, or simply enjoy lounging around as classical melodies that fill the air. It's a delightful trait that adds a touch of whimsy to the robust persona of pit bulls.

The temperament of pit bulls is often under the scanner, given the breed's turbulent history; however, many pit bulls score high on temperament tests, reflecting their affectionate, friendly nature. It's a testament to the breed's potential to be a loving family pet when raised in a nurturing, responsible environment.

Retraining possibility is resilience of pit bulls is awe-inspiring. Many of these dogs, even those rescued from adverse situations, have been successfully re-trained and integrated into loving homes. Their ability to overcome past traumas and embrace a life of love and security is a heartwarming testament to the breed's adaptability and the transformative power of love and patience. For effective re-training of your dog, rely on a *Heavy-Duty Dog Leash* that provides the strength and durability needed to handle powerful breeds.

The physical attributes of pit bulls, their strength, loyalty, and distinct appearance are awe-inspiring. These dogs carry a unique blend of muscular features that means that they are powerful dogs! There are some key points about pit bulls:

Temperament:

- ❖ *Affectionate and Loyal*: Pit Bulls are known for their loyalty and affection towards their families. They often form strong bonds with their owners and can be very loving companions.
- ❖ *Playful*: They tend to be energetic and playful, making them great companions for children.

Trainability:

- ❖ *Intelligence*: Pit Bulls are intelligent dogs and can be trained effectively with positive reinforcement techniques.
- ❖ *Eager* to *please*: They often have a strong desire to please their owners, which can make training easier.

Socialization:

- ❖ *Early Socialization:* It's crucial to socialize Pit Bulls from a young age to ensure that they are well-adjusted and comfortable around other pets and people.
- ❖ *Supervision* with *children*: While many Pit Bulls are gentle with kids, supervision is important, especially with younger children, to ensure safe interactions.

Exercise Needs:

- ❖ *High Energy*: They require regular exercise and mental stimulation to prevent boredom, which can lead to behavioral issues.
- ❖ *These dogs have strong muscles in their body:* With consistent training, socialization, and proper care, Pit Bull Terriers can be wonderful family pets. It's important for potential owners to understand the breed's needs and to commit to providing a loving, structured environment.

Supervision with Children:

- ❖ While many Pit Bulls are gentle with kids, supervision is important, especially with younger children, to ensure safe interactions.
- ❖ With constituent training, socialization, and proper care, Pit Bull Terriers can be wonderful family pets. It's important for potential owners to understand the breed's needs and to commit to providing a loving, structured environment!

Important: Tia Torre is *a famous woman* who took care of *200 Pit Bulls* in *California* at the *Villalobo ranch.* Tia has two daughters, Tania and Mariah who have been a great support for her. Wolves and Pit Bulls were portrayed as society's cast-off canines in full force, and Tia went on fighting to prove that they are gentle and loving animals. Tia created "The Pit Bull Support Group "with the Los Angeles City Animal Services which provided services to anyone who owned Pit Bull or Pit Mix. The Villalobos Rescue Center was not just a rescue for dogs, but it was quickly turning into a rescue for humans as well. However, after Villalobos was on the brink of shutting down in Los Angeles, Tia made the decision in 2010 to move the entire Villalobos Rescue Center to New Orleans!

Tania is Tia's oldest daughter that faced a lot of tragedy as a child yet shares the same love for animals as her mom. In her late teens, Tania was an assistant animal trainer in the film industry. She would find herself in such places as the Mongolian desert with a pack of wolves, or the jungles of Costa Rica with the entire animal cast of "The Jungle Book." Tania has remained the constant in Tia's life. Tania and her siblings found themselves as permanent fixtures at Villalobos, the largest Pit Bull rescue in the country. She is also the author of" Lulu & Clementine," a children's book inspired by one of her dogs, Lulu, and beloved daughter, Salen-Wolf.

Maria was born into the Pit Bull world and got her first Pit Bull L.A. when she was big enough to hold a leash. Growing up, she was very spirited. She

has an innate desire to please, training helps them learn acceptable behavior and leads to a happier, more confident pet. Their instinct is to be friendly, courageous, and never timid.

Chapter 2
Training Dogs at Various States

The barks no more have been in a state of constant flux, shifting between "In Stock" and: Sold Out" nearly every week, and it's also amassed tons of loyal followers! Dogs used to bark up a storm at the smallest of noises. Now, after just one week of using this gadget to prevent your pets from misbehaving! The following states in America have excellent and the best professional dog trainers:

1.Alabama	Brooke McCarley	205-745-3933
2.Alaska	Sandy K.Tundra	206-752-3647-
3. Arizona	Kennedi Travis	605 680-3263
4. Arkansas	Kasey & Frank	479-305-3366
5. California	Andrew Pena	510-629-9494
6. Colorado	Pinna Clek	719-400-8553
7. Connecticut	Jim Stile	518-646-6731
8. Delaware	Kaitlyn B.	860-491-2202
9. Florida	Van Hendrix	305-904-5577
10.Georgia	Sandice Thrasher	706-227-9847
11.Hawaii	Maria H.	808-476-9647
12.Idaho	Taylor & Clayton	404-275-4618
13.Illinois	Julie	815-568-0484
14.Indiana	Mutts	724-717-3007
15.Iowa	Natasha LaUx	319-509-9293
16.Kansas	Kari Ola	816-832-8285
17.Kentucky	Garrett Young	606-775-0550
18.Louisiana	Denise Landin	225-767-8731
19.Maine	Jonathan Wong	614-855-4636
20.Maryland	Fluent	207-619-3007
21.Massachusetts	Lisa Bert	978-387-8377
22.Michigan	Lene Beach	305-846-7841
23.Minnesota	Michael & Lydia O'Leary	877-500-2275
24.Mississippi	Lariy Bea Otte	269-694-6002
25.Missouri	Alex Hans	505-660-0486
26.Montana	Belgin Malinois	505-400-9234
27.Nebraska	Susan Bartman	402-537-3054

28.Nevada	Derek Lissette	877-500-2275
29.New Hampshire	Michael Luevano	877-Bad Dogs
30.New Jersey	Jim Stile	518-646-6002
31.New Mexico	Renee Bolz	505-278-5348
32.New York	Anthony Cietek	518-365-4633
33.New Carolina	Liz Machaffie	505-278-5348
34.North Dakota	Marci Johnson	701-987-1250
35.Ohio	Christine Allison	614-706-1828
36.Oklahoma	Dana Banda	760-607-7690
37.Oregon	Cynthia Morales & John Colageo	760-277-2490
38.Pennsylvania	Michael & Alison Nezbeth	410-739-9903
39.Rhode Island	Lorrie	401-249-4200
40.South Carolina	Jamie	910-988-5220
41.South Dakota	Kelly	605-622-0481
42.Tennessee	Jessica	615-437-5115
43.Texas	Ankita Puri	972-832-9100
44.Utah	Ashley	801-614-2259
45.Vermont	Ian Grant	802-730-6484
46.Virgina	Ethan	571-404-6345
47.Washington	Paul Sheinberg	510-405-4166
48.West Virgina	Brant Weller	504-227-4691
49.Wisconsin	Donna Cutler-Landsman	608-213-5304
50.Wyoming	Karen Pryor-Sabine	307-272-9762

You can watch the professional dog trainer, *Mr. Cesar Millan,* on the television documentary series on many dogs that he trained to be better behavior in America.

Chapter 3
Dog Training

The person's dogs can receive different types of training,

- ❖ Puppy training
- ❖ Adolescent dog training
- ❖ Adult dog training
- ❖ Senior dog training
- ❖ Aggressive attacking dog training
- ❖ Weight reduction dog training
- ❖ Friendly dog to dog training
- ❖ Learning to love children and teens training
- ❖ Learning to play correctly in the city's parks on a daily basis
- ❖ The owner learns to collect their dog's poops correctly
- ❖ Learn their dog's proper behavior indoors (Their homes)
- ❖ Their dogs play with their friends safely
- ❖ U.S. American military service and train the dogs to serve the military safely
- ❖ The dogs take a daily walk and not be aggressive to a neighbor's dog
- ❖ Dogs do not chase a neighbor's cat
- ❖ Having the proper healthy food menu
- ❖ Their dog's health is 100% when they need help at their veterinarian's clinic
- ❖ Children and teens know how to serve their dog's life
- ❖ The dogs can appropriately use a 6-foot walking leash
- ❖ Their dogs know the different clothing that they can use properly
- ❖ Who are the best dog trainers in various states?
- ❖ How expensive is the dog's training?
- ❖ Where should the dog ride in the automobile?
- ❖ How should the dog owner treat the dog outside during the snowstorms and cold rain?
- ❖ What do dogs need to learn when their owner's home burns down?

How can you train the dog to focus on their behavior to being excellent and terrific on their various behaviors? Check the listing of excellent dog trainers in each state and what topic that they can enforce. Be sure to find and locate the finest state trainer to make your dog to be an outstanding animal.

The owners of the dogs need to use their proper voice and hand movements to regulate the dog's proper behaviors and proper movements. Be absolutely that the dogs do not have any bad habits but have good habits to get along with the house-hold cats. The dog should not fight with the cats to maintain less ferocious looking face and not show their teeth and gums and do not sound their growling sound!

Safety for dogs that should be a high priority and training should be done on everything including in the car, the house, outside and with other dogs!

Certain dog breeds that are generally considered friendly with cats include:

Golden Retrievers: Known for their friendly and calm nature, often accepting cats as housemates:

- Labrador Retrievers: Outgoing and social, can easily get along with cats with early socialization.
- Beagles: Friendly dogs that can develop good relationships with cats if introduced young.
- Basset Hounds: Not over excited over other pets.
- Charles Spaniels: People-oriented and gentle and often good with cats.
- Bichon Frizes: Known for getting along well with other animals.
- Maltese: Small and non-threatening and can easily bond with cats.
- Pugs: They can become friends with cats if allowed to interact.

Chapter 4
Puppy's Lessons

Dogs can get into accidents and need to be safe when they walk around. A dog died in Tennessee after it was electrocuted while walking through a puddle outside a Walmart store in Knoxville. The incident occurred on Monday Morning (January 6, 2025) when the pup walked through a puddle and suddenly 'yelped' and lost consciousness, according to a woman who witnessed the event and reported it to the Knoxville Police Department. Despite the attempts by the woman and other people to receive the dog, their efforts were unsuccessful, and it died. The woman who reported this incident said that the dog was electrocuted because she personally felt the shock according to the Knoxville Police Department spokesperson Scott Erland in an email to USA Today on Tuesday. Electrocution is likely due to the infrastructure failure.

Hundreds of puppies in as many as 16 states have contracted a mysterious respiratory illness that has spread across the U.S. since August 2024. Some canines have died as a result. A variety of dog breeds have been affected by the illness, which has symptoms that are similar to Canine Infectious Respiratory Disease Complex, or kennel cough. That's a highly contagious respiratory disease, which affects breathing passages and in the dog's lungs. While the illness mimics the kennel cough, its symptoms do not diminish with the kennel cough treatments. Humans and other pets are not believed to be at risk from illness. What's causing the illness-which doesn't yet have a name or is unknown. However, researchers in New Hampshire say that they have identified a pathogen, an organism that causes disease in a host that is causing the illness, NBC News recently reported this dog's problem.

The researchers described the pathogen as a "funky bacterium" that may be able to defeat canine immune systems. It was discovered by genetic sequencing of samples from 70 dogs, according to scientists at the University of New Hampshire's Veterinary Diagnosis Laboratory and the Hubbard Center for Genome Studies. However; even though a bacteria or virus is found in a sick dog, it doesn't mean the pathogen is what's causing the disease according to Dr. Jason Stull, an assistant professor of the veterinary preventive medicine at Ohio State University. To collect more information, the American Veterinary Medical Association has asked the local vets to report on the cases that they encounter. According to the report the following states have the illness:

1. Washington
2. Oregon
3. Idaho
4. California
5. Colorado
6. Illinois
7. Ohio
8. Pennsylvania
9. New York
10. Connecticut
11. Georgia
12. Florida

Nevada is not on the veterinary association's official list of states in which the cases have been recorded. However, a veterinarian in Henderson, Nevade has reported at least four cases. How does the dog illness spread to other dogs? The illness, which causes chronic respiratory problems, is likely spread through close contact and breathing in the same air as an infected animal according to Dr. David Needle, University of New Hampshire's Veterinary Diagnostic Laboratory senior veterinary pathologist.

Figure 31: These puppies can be very healthy as they grow up and received the Hero Dog Award in Nevada in 2004.

How can you protect your dog from respiratory illness?

❖ Avoid boarding your dog in an area with a high number of other infected dogs.

❖ Make sure that your dog is fully vaccinated.

❖ Monitor your dog for the signs of infection and contact a vet as soon as possible if the symptoms occur.

❖ There are three toxic foods for dogs, which Dr. Marty, which one is better known for dogs, kibble or raw eggs or meat or lambs. Dogs sentenced to death brought back to health with the methods of Dr. Marty Goldstein. One of the greatest cases That was ever had is a Rottweiler dog. The dog was given less than 24 hours to live by the referring veterinarian. Dogs don't need to see the doctor in person to get the benefits of do-it-at-home to remember to let the puppy to represent other dogs to mimic the puppy.

❖ You need to know that a common type of dog food found in every pet store in America is missing a critical vitamin that your dog needs to have a healthy heart.

❖ If you have a dog, you need to know the five preservatives that can damage the dog's health by not being able to digest the bad foods such as:

> 1. Butylated hydroxytoluene
>
> 2. BTH
>
> 3. BHA
>
> 4. Propylene glycol
>
> 5. GMO

❖ Good dog food has a small number of veggies and a small number of fruits to mimic a natural dog's diet.

❖ Corn and soy are not healthy got the dogs not too energetic. They are found in many canned dog foods!

❖ Coloring is used to make dog food more appealing to us, not the dogs who eat it and those coloring chemicals are not good for your dog's body over time. One reason is that dyes do not add to their food's value and clean, healthy, natural diet is demanding by eliminating dyes in their foods.

Are wild wolves making our domestic dogs? According to research, our dogs are not from an extinct gray wolfs species. Since 2008 Zsofia Viranyi, an ethologist at the Wolf Science Center in Austria, and her colleagues have been raising the two species to figure out what makes a dog a dog and a wolf a wolf. There is no evidence that dogs can come from wolves!

Chapter 5
Dog's Adolescent Lessons

Adolescent dogs need to learn obedience training, behavior modification, aggressive behavior, difficulty walking on a leash, excessive humping on people, door bolting or escaping, indoor potty accidents, aggression towards people and other dogs, biting or snapping children and adults. A trainer can use science-based methods to address obedience, socialization, and behavioral concerns that's tailored to your dog's unique needs. An adolescent dog needs to learn to sit, to jump, and to lay down to rest or sleep. Your dog needs to learn how to be your best friend! A great dog trainer will solve the dog's problems that allow them to live life to the fullest again while regaining control and confidence.

Just about everyone knows to be prepared to deal with the crazy or relentless puppy behavior; but way fewer dog owners, it seems, have been warned about the other challenging period in a dog's life lie during adolescence! A quick Google search on the topic produces results that peppered with words like "surviving," "dealing with," and "misbehaviors. "When dealing with teenage dogs the teaching list will get long and more difficult and worse! Goodness, it sounds horrible! It's true that this period involves a ton of changes to your dog's biological, physical, and psychological makeup. By extension, the adolescent dog's behavior is affected in a great fashion. It's also true that there are times when this transformation is ac-companied by some challenging moments; but rest assured that it's not all doom and gloom! For every challenging feature of canine adolescence, there is an equally awesome element that makes this a very special time. The adolescent period typically begins around six months of age and will be over when a dog reaches physical maturity around two to three years old. The most pronounced behavioral issues will be noticed between six to 12 months old. Keep in mind that although hormones have a lot to do with adolescent changes, they're not the only thing responsible for some of the behaviors that you may see (Even neutered dogs will exhibit these behaviors). Your dog's brain is growing and developing, and the apparent quirkiness of the process is all perfectly natural. As a trainer and a person who is currently in the adolescent trenches with my Border 'Terrier; I can testify that it's not all bad. Here are some facts about canine adolescence that you may not be aware of, and some tips that you can hope will help guide you through this challenging time with your teenaged dog.

1.   *Bonding with your teenage dog is important:* The foundation of your relationship with you dog is taking shape and getting stronger. If you've had your adolescent dog since puppyhood, time has been on your side. You've had several months to get to know each other and to build a bond. That's a very good thing. It's always much easier to forgive and to exercise patience with someone or a dog that we care deeply about. So, while the puppyhood antics may have pushed your buttons and left you scrambling for a moment's peace for several weeks in a row, adolescent shenanigans can be surprisingly easier to tolerate, thanks to that bond. You'll still need to draw deeply from the patience pool during this time; but by now your dog will have improved in other departments:

     ❖ The dog knows some basic clues thanks to your training
     ❖ The dog will be housetrained
     ❖ The dog's needs won't always require an immediate response on your part, like when the dog was a young pup.

2.   *Teething is almost done!* Most of the really difficult teething phase occurs before adolescence, and while it doesn't really wrap up until about seven to nine months old, it's not nearly as dramatic as the earlier stages. Some breeds of dogs remain power chewers throughout their adult life; however; and it's important to evaluate and adjust the types of chew toys you're giving your adolescent dog. What was suitable for a five-month-olds puppy might no longer represent a safe option for your dog. What was suitable for a five-month-old puppy that might no longer represent a safe option for your dog's newer and more powerful jaw. For example, if it used to take the dog an hour to work its way through a bulky stick several weeks ago, it might now only last the dog 10 minutes, and the dog should be watched closely, or the dog may now be able to chew off chunks of a chew stick that previously the dog could barely dent.

3.   *Adolescent dogs have different sleeping schedules:* Remember when your puppy used to spend more time asleep than awake? Those days are gone; your teenage dog now seems to have access to an endless supply of energy! If your arm yourself with lots of short, fun training sessions and brain games, you'll fare much better than if you rely solely on physical exercise to tire out your young dog. Besides, you'll want to avoid any serious physical activity that involves sudden stops and turns or jumps and bounces. Your dog's skeletal structure isn't quite done taking

shape yet and you'll want to protect your dog's joints until at least 12 to 18 months of age, depending on your dog's age and his size. Back to sleeping your dog teenage dog will very likely experience some disruptions in your dog's nighttime sleeping pattern which means that you'll also experience a few sleepless nights. Your teen dog will very likely experience a few sleepless nights, and your dog might snooze the entire evening away and just when you're ready to call it a night at 11p.m., your dog suddenly widens awake and be ready to party with you! There's little that you can do to convince your dog to settle down. Don't worry because these episodes will come and go and all that's needed is a little bit of patience and time.

4. *Socializing your teenage dog is important:* Socialization needs to continue because you've done a wonderful job socializing your pup during the sensitive socialization period (before 12 to 16 weeks of age); but it shouldn't stop now that your dog is a teenager. Even if you've just adopted an adolescent dog and your dog's socialization history is unknown, it's important to continue to carefully expose your dog to different places, people, other dogs and different situations (Like riding in a car or truck) while associating these events with something positive. You might notice that your dog may quite suddenly appear wary or even fearful of things or situations that your dog previously had no issue with any problem. This is normal because these moments will come and go several times during adolescence and may last anywhere from a couple of days to a few weeks. Your dog may give a scary fire hydrant a very wide berth during your walk, or your dog might decide that new people or dogs (Or trees or shadows) should be barked at any time. Don't worry because you handle these moments with calmness and patience and understanding that your dog isn't always able to control their emotions during these phases. Don't push or force your dog to confront his fear and don't scold your dog for what may look like rude behavior. Try to give your dog time to process whatever speaks to your dog or dogs. If your dog wants to turn away and avoid the scary things because it's okay, even if your dog barks at anything. Often, just crouching next to your dog and talking with a gentile voice is enough to calm your dog's barking. Some people lay low when they notice their dog is experiencing a fearful phase to opting to avoid situations that cause their dog stress, like busy streets or large crows. When your dog shows signs that your dog is feeling more confident, your dog's activities resume as normal!

5. *Teenage dogs become more interested in going for walks:* Many young puppies balk at wandering too far away from the safety of their home. They'll take a few steps on-leash and then will suddenly slam on the brakes and stand still like a statue. Nature designs them this way, for good reasons. Adolescence serves to create just the opposite:

   1. A biological urge to wander further from the nest and to explore new places.

   2. You'll notice your adolescent dog also has more stamina to keep up with you doing daily walks and your dog enjoys investigating the various scents.

   3. Adventures with your dog now become a lot more fun.

   4. Resist the urge to let your dog off-leash and don't use an extralong leash to walk your dog.

   5. You'll want to maintain this high rate of reinforcement until your dog is an adult dog.

6. *Your dog's training might seem to come and go:* Remember how proud that that you were of your puppy's training results. How quickly does your dog learn to sit, to lie down, to come and leave the owner? Where did all those skills go? If it seems as though your dog has forgotten all of his training, don't worry because your dog really didn't forget all of your dog's memory! The information is still there, floating around in that rapidly developing brain of that dog. Your dog is just having a bit of trouble accessing all that knowledge right now. This too will return to normal when your dog's done with the teenage phase. Keep teaching, keep rewarding, and keep breathing. All of the efforts will pay off later.

7. *How can a puppy potty train outside of the apartment:* The basic methods for potty training are the same anywhere; but there are a few extra challenges when house training a young dog in an apartment requires skills. Potty training a puppy is an exercise in diligence consistency and patience, requiring owners to keep a close eye on their dog's body language, do their best to prevent accidents from happening and provide rewards when the puppy relieves themselves. So, how do these things apply when it comes to how to potty train a puppy by coming the same. The biggest issue when potty training a puppy is the distance between the living space and the yard. If you start moving the movement that shows the slightest sign of needing to go out, the time it takes to navigate all of that is often too much for a young dog's bladder. If you can't consistently make it on time, it can be very

difficult to teach the puppy where it's appropriate to puppy. A brilliant plan is for the owner to have an apartment or house with a large closed in back yard for their dog's potting.

Figure 32. The puppies require a professional trainer to help the young dogs to play with the children and their parents. The young dogs obtained the Hero Dog Award in 2005.

If it seems as though your dog has forgotten all of his training, don't worry because your dog really didn't forget all of your dog's memory! The information is still there, floating around in that rapidly developing brain of that dog. Your dog is just having a bit of trouble accessing all that knowledge right now. This too will return to normal when your dog's done with the teenage phase. Keep teaching, keep rewarding, and keep breathing. All of the efforts will pay off later.

7. How can a puppy potty train outside of the apartment: The basic methods f or potty training are the same anywhere; but there are a few extra challenges when house training a young dog in an apartment requires skills. Potty training a puppy is an exercise in diligence consistency and patience, requiring owners t o keep a close eye on their dog's body language, do their best to prevent acci dents from happening and provide rewards when the puppy relieves themselves.

So, how do these things apply when it comes to how to potty train a puppy by coming the same. The biggest issue when potty training a puppy is the dist ance between the living space and the yard. If you start moving the movement that shows the slightest sign of needing to go out, the time it takes to navigate all of that is often too much for a young dog's bladder. If you can't consistentl y make it on time, it can be very difficult to teach the puppy where it's appro priate to puppy. A brilliant plan is for the owner to have an apartment or hou se with a large closed in back yard for their dog's potting.

Figure 32. The puppies require a professional trainer to help the young dogs to play with the children and their parents. The young dogs obtained the Hero Dog Award in 2005.

Chapter 6
Dog's Adult Lessons

More than just dog obedience training, you need to develop a good and strong relationship with your dog! Many adult dogs have more knowledgeable behaviors than a younger dog. There are several techniques that are required to use when making adult dogs more loveable and skilled. Can a person teach an adult dog to heel? This can be done by the following:

- ✓ *Start in a low-distraction area:* Begin training in an enclosed space, like your garden or indoors where there are fewer distractions.
- ✓ *Use positive reinforcement:* Reward your adult dog with treats or toys when they follow your cues.
- ✓ *Be patient and consistent:* Don't move too quickly through the training stages and don't neg your dog by constantly repeating the command.
- ✓ *Introduce distractions gradually:* Once your dog is doing well, gradually increase the distance between the dog and the distraction.
- ✓ *Very routine:* Change sides, make turns, make turns, and stop.
- ✓ Start with short walks: When you're ready to take your dog on outdoor walks, start with short stretches of heel walking.
- ✓ Heeling is a useful skill that can help you control your dog's actions and make the walks safer. An adult dog that knows how to heel is less likely to chase other animals, run onto the road and get hit by a car or truck, or eat something harmful.

There are five tips for training your adult dog to walk on a leash without pulling. Walking your dog should be an enjoyable and relaxing activity for both you and your furry dog; However, if your dog pulls on the leash, what should be a peaceful stroll that can quickly become a frustrating and exhausting task. The good news is that with the right approach and tools, you can train your dog to walk calmly by your side without pulling. In this blog post, you can share the five essential tips to help you and your dog master leash walking, and I will introduce a product that can make the process even smoother.

1. Start with the right equipment: Before you begin training your dog to walk on a leash without pulling. It's crucial to have the right equipment. The type of leash and hardness that you use can significantly impact your training success. Many dog owners start with a standard collar and leash; but these can actually encourage pulling and lead to choking or discomfort for your dog. Instead of a collar, opt for a no-pull harness which is designed to distribute pressure more evenly across your dog's body, reducing the risk of injury and making it easier to guide your dog without force. The favorite no-pull hardness is the "Shawn Company Essential Hardness" as it features three different lash attachment points, allowing you to find the best option for controlling your dog's movements. It's no pull technology discourages the pulling, making your walks more enjoyable and safer.

2. *Use positive reinforcement:* Positive reinforcement is one of the most effective training methods when it comes to teaching your dog good behavior. This involves rewarding your dog with treats, praise, or affection whenever they walk calmly by your side without pulling on the leash. The idea is to make your dog associate walking politely with positive outcomes. Whenever your dog starts to pull, stop walking immediately. Wait for your dog to return to your side, then reward them with a treat or praise. Over time, your dog will learn that staying by your side is the best way to earn rewards. Transitioning from a collar to a harness can also make positive reinforcement more effective with a no-pull harness, your dog will be more comfortable and less likely to become frustrated or anxious during training. This comfort can lead to a more relaxed and receptive dog during the training sessions.

3. *Practice patience and consistency:* Training your dog to walk on *a* leash without pulling requires patience and consistency. It's important to remember that the change of behavior doesn't happen overnight. Some dogs may take longer to learn, especially if they've been pulling on the leash for a long time. The key is to stay consistent with your training methods and practice regularly. Start by practicing in your closed-in backyard or a quiet park, then gradually move to a busier area as your dog becomes more confident. If your dog begins to pull when distracted, use the same stop-and-reward technique as before. Consistent practice in different settings will help your dog learn to stay focused and walk politely, no matter what's happening around them.

4. *Introduce distractions gradually:* One thing that needs training is to stop barking and biting a person. The dog is trying to tell you something important. Barking is more than just noise. Your dog is trying to communicate and understanding why they're barking is the first step managing it effectively. In this episode, it's your dog trying to tell you the following things:

The real reasons that your dog bark is from: boredom or excitement.

❖ The barks are from fear, territorial instincts, and even attention seeking.

- ❖ Whether your dog is a chatterbox or just has the occasional barking spree which can bring a little more peace and quiet to your home.
- ❖ Adult dogs can always be hungry during the morning, lunch, and dinner or even evening.
- ❖ Adult dogs may need a sweater during the winter when walking outside together with a beautiful 6-foot and colorful leash!
- ❖ Adult dogs love to gather their energy and play with their household children and their parents.

Chapter 7
Dog's Senior Lessons

Senior dogs typically enjoy gentle activities like short walks, sniffing around on scent walks, playing with puzzle toys to stimulate their minds, cuddling with their owners, receiving treats, and engaging in low-impact games like gentle fetch with soft toys, as their physical capabilities that may be reduced with age like being patient and respecting their limitations while providing mental stimulation and companionship. There are key points about senior dog activities:

- ❖ *Low-impact exercise*: Short, leisurely walks, allowing them to sniff and explore at their own pace, are preferred over long, vigorous runs.
- ❖ *Mental stimulation*: Puzzle toys, treat-dispensing toys, and scent games can keep their minds active even as their physical abilities decline.
- ❖ *Cuddling and companionship*: The senior dogs often crave close contact and attention from their owner and kids.
- ❖ *Gentle* play: Soft toys for fetching or simple tug-of-war can be fun for the older dogs.
- ❖ *Consistent routine*: Maintaining a predictable schedule can provide comfort and security for the senior dogs.

Senior dogs can suffer from age-related cognitive decline, including cognitive dysfunctional syndrome, which is all the more reason to provide lots of enrichment opportunities. As your dog grows older, they'll experience many changes, from gray hair to loss of mobility, vision, and hearing changes, and more susceptibility to medical issues. While some changes may be more noticeable than others, it's important to be aware of everything that you can expect from your ageing pup. What changes that I can expect from senior dogs:

- ✓ Thinning and greying fur in senior dogs.
- ✓ Reduced activity and mobility in senior dogs.
- ✓ Weight changes in older dogs.
- ✓ Susceptibility to the temperature in older dogs.
- ✓ Loss of hearing and vision changes.
- ✓ Behavior changes are great.
- ✓ Dental issues become more common.
- ✓ Medical issues are more common.

✓ An older dog acquires more diseases and should visit a veterinarian to resolve their illness.

Almost all House-Dog Rescue of Ohio has always had a soft spot for senior collies, shelties, and collie/sheltie mixes. Foster homes for these dogs are common in Ohio. By fostering can open up a whole new world for older dogs, seniors can have the companionship of a pet without housebreaking, training, or cost. Medical examinations for your dogs are costly and you may consider animal health insurance policy! Senior dogs are beginning to slow down and lose enthusiasm to run around, having fun, playing with toys, and making new dog friends. Do you think that your dog is losing their enthusiasm for riding a car? There is one activity that I have always adored doing with every dog in my life is The Find It Game. Every dog played with it and loved it because they do not get too tired; but have many ways and time to be happier...In America, there are 89.7 million dogs and 73.8 million cats!

Dog's nutritional needs start to change when they reach age 7 and you need to examine your dog's det. There are many brands of dog foods, and you must be willing to study them to study the botanical oils used and the high-quality carbohydrate sources like oatmeal and whole grain wheat. These helps promote mental sharpness and healthy energy in senior dogs. You may even an average increase in activity level over 20% when you feed it to your older dog plus, this is easily digestible dog food that is made with real chicken as the number1 ingredient to help keep the dog coming back meal after meal.

Chewing is also always fun. Does your dog have a window seat? A lot of dogs enjoy watching people and animals from the window. Try nose work that you can teach your dog to find specific orders or just do half the time and practice that your dog "wait" while you hide tiny stinky treats all around one room, then tell the dog "Go sniff" and watch your dog turn that room upside down finding every last one. I thought their lazy old 100-pound dog to sniff things out, and the dog may not have been as fast and wild as your young lab; but an owner did have a great methodical nose and the dog just loved it. There really wasn't much else that would really get the dog up and moving and interested, so it was a lifesaver in the dog's older years. The senior dogs get tired more quickly now, you can explore other activities to enjoy together such as:

➢ *Short*walks: Instead of long walks or runs, try going for shorter walks or runs at a pace that suits the dog. This will still provide exercise while being gentler on the dog's energy levels.

> ➢ *Indoor games:* Engage in indoor games like fetch with soft toys or hide-and-seek. These activities can be adjusted to the dog's energy level and are perfect for spending quality time indoors.
> ➢ Puzzle toys: Invest in puzzle toys that stimulate the dog's mind and keep the dog entertained. These toys can help keep the dog's mind sharp and provide mental stimulation, which is just as important as physical activity.

I did an Easter egg hunt in the backyard or inside the house and I hid some treats and allowed the dog to find them! You can use many other dog toys to entertain your dog.

Be sure that the senior dogs are protected from house fires. About 40,000 pets die in residential fires each year, mostly from smoke inhalation, and 500,000 pets are affected overall. The Philadelphia firefighter, Jen Leary said that you'll see enough people who have just lost everything having to make bad decisions about what they're going to do with their pets. The Salvation Army is on the scene giving out blankets, the Red Cross providing emergency shelter, and medics attending to human injuries; but there are no resources for the other members of the family and their pets. The Red Cross can arrange temporary housing for the displaced residents, but not for their pets. Most of the time, people left them in their burned-out dwelling or gave them to some neighbor or stranger on the street that they didn't know or had to surrender them to the animal control people. The Red Paw Emergency Relief Team responds to emergency alerts for fires, explosions, gas leaks, water main breaks and when the building collapses. The Red Paw found dogs and cats.

In the building and homes. In 2011, the nonprofit Red Paw Emergency Relief Team provided search and rescue, shelter, and emergency veterinary care for the animals injured in fires and other disasters. The Red Paw response vehicle is sent out by the on-duty dispatcher, either the one based at a Team's home in south Philadelphia or the one at Engine 22 in northeast Philadelphia. There are two full-time responders, four per diem responders, and three volunteer responders. Each is a firefighter or military veteran. At the scene, the Red Paw response vehicle is sent out by the on-duty dispatcher, the one based at Jen Leary's home.

There are 7 dog breeds that are perfect for homebodies and couch lovers. For those people who cherish a quiet, laid-back lifestyle, certain dog breeds are more than just pets, they're the perfect companions. These dogs thrive indoors, require minimal exercise and enjoy being with their owners in smaller spaces like apartments or homes with limited rooms. Whether you're a city dweller, introvert or simply someone who enjoys staying in, these breeds are ideal for you! Let's dive into your couch and keep you company while you relax. Here are the perfect dogs that you should get:

1. *Japanese Chin:* This dog is the quintessential lapdog, and for good reason! With their gentle, affectionate personality, they make perfect companions for the pet parents who prefer a peaceful home life. These dogs are incredibly intelligent and independent, which means that they enjoy spending time with their humans but won't demand constant attention. Whether it's lounging by your side or entertaining themselves with their playful nature, the Japanese Chins adapt well to homes with the limited space and low exercise needs. Their minimal exercise requirements make them ideal for those who don't want to spend much time outdoors. A few short walks and some indoor playtimes are all they need to stay happy. Despite their small stature, they pack a big personality, often surprising their owners with bursts of energy when they feel playful. If you're someone who enjoys having a calm, affectionate dog around, the Japanese Chin will be a perfect fit with you and your home with the family. Adaptable to apartment life or cozy homes, these dogs are low-maintenance and always ready for some quiet time with their owner. The dog is not the type to bark unnecessarily, making them great for anyone looking for a calm atmosphere. With their elegant appearance and sweet nature, this dog will keep you and your family during the dog's overwhelming activity in your space.

Figure 33: Japanese Chin can live with the owner very quietly and received the Hero Dog Award in 2021 in Japan.

2. *Greyhound:* This dog might surprise you as one of the best indoor dogs for homebodies. They are known for their speed and agility. These graceful dogs are surprisingly relaxed when it comes to indoor life. After their short bursts of outdoor

exercise, Greyhounds are content to settle down on the couch and nap the day away. With their laid-back attitude, they fit perfectly in smaller spaces like apartments and are ideal for owners who lead calm, peaceful lives. Through they have a racing dog, the Greyhounds don't require much exercise beyond a daily walk, and they adapt easily to a quiet home environment. If you're looking for a dog that will enjoy lounging as much as you do, a Greyhound will fit right in! Their slender frame and low energy make them ideal for smaller homes, and they love to rest in a cozy spot by your feet. Despite their athletic build, these dogs tend to have a"couch potato" side. You can implement this action by purchasing a dog bed that fits your dog's size! Greyhounds are calm, intelligent, and affectionate, making them wonderful companions for those who prefer to stay in and unwind.

Figure 34: Greyhound (Adult) is a great dog for the homeless person and rece ived their Hero Dog Award in 2022.

3. *Papillion:* This dog is small and spirited and is a fantastic choice for homebodies who want to bite more personality in their pet. While they are playful and energetic, they aren't demanding when it comes to exercise. A few short walks and indoor play sessions are all that they need. Papillons thrive in smaller spaces and adapt well to a quieter environment, making them perfect companions for city dwellers or those in apartments. These dogs were originally bred as tatters to get rid of pests in people's homes. Their process was to hunt rats and tire them out until exhaustion and then make their final move. They were represented in many famous painters' works, from Titian and Goya Rubens and even Rembrandt! This breed of dogs gets very attracted to their owners and are prone to developing separation anxiety when separated from them. The Papillion are a breed of dog that seems to be growing in popularity and for good reasons-they are amazing little dogs, and they are highly intelligent and active

dogs and enjoy participating in activities with the whole family, indoors or outdoors. They are affectionate and responsive to the people that they have bonded with, which their humans are away for long periods of time. These dogs are very playful and affectionate. Widely known as great companion dogs, they have the spirit and energy to keep up with active families that pick them up and carry them around. This breed of dogs is prone to allergies, seizures, and dental diseases.

Figure 35: Papillion (Adult) are small, but playful dogs that love the indoor activities in the small apartment and received their Hero Dog Award in 2023.

These dogs do not like to swim, and you should not expect them to participate! However, they like flyball and rally. They like to sleep between 12 to 14 hours a day. These dogs are often busy with various activities, from playing and exploring to training and socializing. These attractive breeds are many actresses' possessions because they walk their dogs all over Hollywood!

4. *Chihuahua*: These dogs are tiny and are liked by many people around the world:

❖ Height

5-8 inches

❖ Weight

Not exceed 6 pounds

❖ Life expectancy

14-16 years

These dogs are great with children and adults who walk them. These dogs were recognized in Mexico as a famous dog that were noted in the mid-19m century and officially recognized by the American Kennel Club in 1904. There are many different breeds:

- ✓ Mexican hairless dog
- ✓ Chihuahua dog
- ✓ Long-haired Chihuahua dog
- ✓ Long-haired Chihuahua dog

It has been estimated that over 25,000 Chihuahua dogs were discovered in America. Of the dogs that American people own dogs, but 4% own Chihuahua dogs. The Chihuahua is a generally healthy breed with an expected lifespan of 14 to 16 years, but some have been known to make it well into their 20s. They are one of the longest-lived dog breeds. However, like all purebred dogs, the Chihuahuas can be predisposed to certain health conditions such as:

- ➢ Collapsing the trachea
- ➢ Congestive heart failure
- ➢ Hypoglycemia
- ➢ Luxating Patella (Dislocated kneecap]
- ➢ Patent Ductus Arteriosus (Congenital heart valve defect)
- ➢ Hydrocephalus (Fluid buildup in the brain]
- ➢ Cataracts
- ➢ Glaucoma
- ➢ Dental Defects
- ➢ Obesity
- ➢ Due to their size, Chihuahuas can also have a hard time regulating their body temperature. They have a very low body mass and need extra care to keep warm, especially in colder climates during the winter months. Their small

stature also makes them fragile. Unfortunately, these dogs have been known to sustain fractures just from jumping off the furniture or engaging in the plays. Extra caution should be taken to help prevent injuries. While not every of these dogs will be impacted by one of these conditions, pet insurance is always a good thing to have to help with veterinary expenses. Especially in cases of accidents or emergencies. There are several unique attributes that help define this breed. Here's what you can expect from a purebred dog. These dogs are generally regarded as the world's smallest dogs. They are in a class known as toy breeds. The Chihuahuas typically weigh just 3 to 6 pounds and stand between 5 and 8 inches tall. They come in a variety of colors with markings that can include bi-color and tri-color variations. The Chihuahua coats can be either smooth (short) or long. In addition to their signature small stature, these dogs have other distinguishing characteristics that help set them apart from their big expressive eyes and pointed ears to their uniquely shaped heads. Dogs tend to have one of two head shapes:

> Round and apple-like or
> Elongated and deer-like

These dogs are loyal, feisty, and quick-witted dogs. They tend to cling to their owners but be wary of strangers and other dogs. They are also very vigilant and protective of their owners and their space; they have no problem standing up for themselves, even if it means staring down a much larger dog or barking at a stranger on the street. While some of these dogs that were socialized early or raised with other dogs will enjoy some canine company, overall, the breed is not particularly social. They like to be with their owners, preferably curled up in the owners' lap. Having a good training plan to bond with your dog while cultivating an enjoyable way to be safer and happier dog. One of the top dog training benefits is creating a way of communication, allowing your pet to understand what you want from them. Training provides mental stimulation enrichment, reducing unwanted destructive behaviors like chewing the owner's shoes, and digging in their garden is actually just a natural dog behavior. Dogs have no concept of the right or wrong, and what's considered a 'bad' behavior is very subjective by training your dog to redirect behaviors (Like chewing on toys), you set them up for success. Training builds your dog's confidence, creating a calmer and more self-assured pet. Most importantly you need to strengthen your connection with your dog. It is a great way to bond with your dog. It is something that your dog will look forward to doing with you and strengthen your connection.

1. *Why is dog training important? A* dog that has been trained to tolerate being handled can be more thoroughly checked in the veterinary exams, leading to more efficient care. Training your dog creates safety for your dog in the different situations that you may come across. If your dog picks up something possibly dangerous on a walk, you can use the 'drop it' cue to prevent them from eating it. Saving them from a trip to the emergency vet.

2. *How to train your dog and get training tips: Dog* obedience training used to be the norm. The trainers would use force and domination to control the dog's behavior. With the advancements in understanding how dogs learn force-based obedience training is now considered an outdated approach that often causes more harm than good. For example, you're training your dog not to beg but eventually give them a bite of food when they whine. You're giving a reward (access to food) for the behavior that you want to discourage (begging) and reinforcing the behavior.

3. *Does dog training really work?* The simple answer is that positive reinforcement-based dog training naturally shapes your dog's behavior, but it also teaches your dog that training is your dog's fun. Your dog takes on an active role in learning. Punishment or force-based training methods are less effective when trying to raise a modern dog. There is a growing movement to teach dog owners all about early socialization and the value of rewards-based training, and plenty of trainers who employed only positive reinforcement. But in those days, the approach was the subject of debate and derision:

   ❖ Treat-trained mongers that might do what if they knew a biscuit is hidden in your palm, but
   ❖ In those days, the approach was the subject of debate and derision might treat-trained mongers might do what you want if they knew a biscuit is hidden in your palm, but they'd ignore you otherwise. You can teach your dog tough LOVE.

4. Older dog obedience training can be a good idea and whether you recently adopted an adult dog or your canine companion needs a refreshed on the basic commands, training your dog teaches them good behaviors and strengthens your bond: Additionally, despite what you may think, it is possible to train adult

and senior dogs while they might be less impressionable than puppies, older canines have more self-control and can often focus for longer periods of time. Curious about training for dogs? Find lessons on my Purina application or read on to learn training recommendations and how-to-tips. If you're wondering if your dog needs obedience training, consider how serious their problem is. For example, if your dog is generally well-behaved but doesn't always sit still when you want them to, you may or may not want to spend time on you may or may not want to spend time and energy fixing the issue. However, for adult canines who engage in destructive or dangerous behavior, it's recommended that you pursue dog obedience training. Here are common examples of troublesome behaviors that can be improved through good training:

✓ *Leash-pulling.* Walking calmly on a leash by your side doesn't come naturally to most dogs (Especially If your adult dog never learned that they could learn to walk without pulling.

✓ *Digging.* A dog who loves to dig can be destructive to your yard. By ensuring that they get enough exercise and mental stimulation, you may be able to curb the dog's behavior:

✓ *Aggression.* An aggressive dog may exhibit threatening behavior towards strangers, family members or other animals. If your pet is aggressive, they likely need intervention from an animal behaviorist in addition to training. Also, contact your veterinarian to rule out an underlying medical condition.

✓ *How to obedience-train an older dog at home:* if you want to train your older canine, here's an overview of basic dog behaviors that can be taught at home:

1. To teach your dog to sit, start by making eye contact with them.
2. With the dog standing, hold a treat or kibble in front of their nose. This is called lurking.
3. Move the treat or kibble over their head towards their back, creating a natural sit. Move slowly and keep the treat or kibble directly in front of their nose.
4. When your dog is reliably following the treat or kibble into a sit, that you can then start using your knowledge to praise them.
5. Once the dog is reliably following the treat or kibble into a sit, you can then start using your empty hand in the same movement. Always reinforce the behavior with a treat or kibble and praise the dog.
6. When your dog is consistently sitting without the treat or kibble, add a verbal cue, such as **"sit."**

✓ *A senior dog program:* This is specially designed to meet the needs of older dogs. The program focuses on strengthening a reasonable range of motion, improving mobility and body awareness and integrating movement patterns that will be helpful navigating life. All while being mindful of compressive forces and impact on your dog! By focusing on moderate weight bearing, paying attention to alignment and staying in the mid-range, the trainer can improve the strength and stability without aggravating arthritic conditions in the limbs and spine. Mobility focused on exercise concentrates on real life demands that your dog is likely to meet. While at the same time avoiding excessive range that can unintentional-ally result in soreness and avoidance. Senior Specific guidelines for modifying prop setup and reward delivery are included in the PDE The puppy training lessons with your young dog are just the first step in a great training journey that can reach a high-level obedience and control.

✓ *Behavior Modification:* Through balanced training and counter-conditioning the excellent trainers can modify the dog's behavior: Behavior modification is the most complex training process that the good trainers offer but they are also trying to change the way the dog looks at the world.

✓ *Personal Protection:* in an age where personal security is of high importance and where crime is prevalent, the most effective way to defend your family and home is with an effective home protection dog! More than just dog obedience training, develop training that will develop your relationship with your dog!

✓ *Longest living dog breed:* When the skilled trainer thinks that large dog breeds with image of strong, majestic, and loyal companions immediately comes to mind. These gentle giants bring love, joy, and protection into your lives, but sadly, they often have shorter lifespans than their smaller counter parts. For many dog lovers, this reality can be heart-breaking. However, not all big dogs are destined for a brief stay! Some large breeds defy the odds, boasting impressively long lifespans, often living 12 to 14 years or more. The longest living large dog breeds that bring size and personality to the table and give you plenty of cherished years to create memories together. Whether it's the fiercely loyal Anatolian Shepherd, the agile Australian Cattle dog, or the elegant Borzoi, these breeds prove that the size doesn't always dictate longevity:

1. *Anatolian Shepherd:* This breed blends strength, independence, and remarkable longevity. Originating in Turkey as a livestock guardian, these dogs are built to a dog with a large, muscular, and powerful livestock guardian dog breed originating in foreign country and bred for millennia to protect flocks from wolves and bears, they are loyal, alert, and protective. The appearance:

all and weighs 110 to

Figure 36: Anatolian Shepherd (Adult) is a remarkable dog to their owner and received the Hero Dog Award in 2000.

They are known for their guarding instincts and are fiercely loyal. They are not typically outgoing dogs and can be aloof even towards their owners. Trust is earned with these dogs, and it is not a master-servant relationship, but rather a partnership is based on mutual respect. This dog is available in different colors and variations, such as the Kangal, akbosh, and Karabash.

2. *Neapolitan Mastiff:* This dog has a lifespan of 10 to 15 years, with some even exceeding 18 years in age; medium breeds typically live for 10 to 13 years. The latter

Figure 37: Napolitan Mastijf (Adult) is a rapidly growing dog that sometimes gets cancer despite receiving the Hero Dog Award.

3. ***Beagle***: This floppy-eared doe-eyed beagles are often regarded as the perfect family pet. A record holder for the longest beagles. Their nutritional value of these foods is a major contributor to low energy, digestive issues, joint discomfort, bad breath, smelly or mushy poop, itchy skin, and a host of other common problems in this dog. However, after years of studying the issue and even writing a best-selling book, Dr. Marty says that he has finally found a way to fight back. Luckily, by recognizing the early signs of danger, he has helped countless dogs enhance their well-being. This realization led this veterinarian to recognize the exact things that take about 2 minutes a day, and it can have a major impact on your dog's quality life. There are several foods that are toxic to this dog:

   ✓ ***Macadamia nuts***: Not only do they have a high content oil that can irritate a dog's stomach, but also for unknown reasons, this nut can be toxic. According to the veterinarians a dose of about two macadamia nuts per dog's pound can lead to a temporary inability to walk. The worst-case scenario is causing paralysis, and the dogs can suffer severe weakness, nausea, and diarrhea that will require hospitalization.

✓ *Cooked Bones*: The cooking process makes bones more brittle than raw ones, making them more likely to splinter when

✓ a dog chews them! Potential outcomes include broken teeth, mouth injuries, constipation, and most concerning thing-a blockage or perforation in the intestinal track. That can also cause peritonitis, or inflammation around the stomach tissue.

✓ *Leeks, Onions, and Garlic:* These vegetables are part of the allium family that can injure the RBC in dogs, meaning that they can make the dog anemic! The dog can get hemolytic anemia, which requires a hospital trip. Complicating matters that can take days before the anemia is revealed.

✓ *Dairy*: Most dogs are lactose-intolerant and can lead to a variety of stomach issues. Subsequent vomiting, diarrhea, and other gastrointestinal problems may require hospitalization.

✓ *Bacon*: You may not feel bad after that hot bacon after inhaling a plate of bacon, but it's even worse for your dog. This breakfast treat contains a load of FAT that can lead to pancreatitis (An inflamed pancreatitis) and other problems:

1. *Pancreatitis*: Bacon can cause pancreatitis, which is an inflammation of the pancreas. This disease can be life-threatening to your dog.

2. *Dehydration*: Bacon's high sodium content can lead to bloating and dehydration.

3. *Gastrointestinal issues:* Bacon can cause diarrhea, vomiting, constipation, gas, and abdominal pain.

4. *Other health issues:* Bacon can also cause lethargy, weight gain, and diabetes.

5. *What can you do if your dog eats bacon:*

   ❖ *Bloat*: Bacon is a high sodium food, meaning that it has a high salt content. Salty foods can result in a condition in your dog's stomach expanding with air called bloat. This is also caused by excessive dehydration that makes the dog drink too much water. Bloat can cause your dog extreme discomfort and could result in damage to the internal organs.

❖ *Inflammation of the pancreas:* Fatty foods and processed meats like bacon can result in an inflamed pancreas or pancreas-titis, a potentially fatal illness.

❖ The greases and fats in bacon prematurely activate the digestive system, which can lead to nausea, vomiting, and diarrhea. Just one piece of bacon can trigger these symptoms, and it may require a trip to the vet.

❖ *Before sharing with your pooch:* Certain human foods can cause adverse reactions in canines, so always consult your veterinarian to determine whether it is safe to add these foods to your pet's diet.

ining the dog's male or

o
e
e
d
w

Figure 38: Beagle (Adult) is a dog with a large brain that can understand many words from humans and received the Hero Dog Award in 2025.

Chapter 8
Dog's Vacation Lessons

Dogs can go to the local beach and play in the sand with the kids and later enter the water with the adults and children. We know thousands of people have adopted pets recently-and people want to make every one of them enjoy their visit their vacation site. The active dogs will swim or learn to ride a surfboard. The young and active dog will visit the owners' winter visit at their cabins in the snowy mountains. They will learn to wear winter clothing to protect their body. During the summer, the dogs will wear protective clothing to hide from the sun rays, rain, and heat. The owner does not like to cover the dog with protective clothing. If the owner with a dog goes fishing in a boat may hesitate to bring his dog along. If the owner has a bicycle with a basket to load their dog for transportation ride. If the dog's tail is wiggling, then they may be happy. If they hide their tail between their hind legs, they are not excited. At friendly hotels, restaurants, and sport events some dogs are happy, and many others are unhappy.

Knoxville is quite paw-silly, the most pet friendly in America. It is true id you're traveling with your dog, you'll find pet-friendly hotels and patios in lots of cities; but the fun shouldn't end there! There's no end to the things to do with your dog in Knoxville and other friendly American cities and small towns.

There are many friendly parks for your dogs to socialize and play with other canine friends. The seven ultimate dog breeds that wear loyalty like a cape. When choosing a dog, many people are looking for a composition who will stay by their síde through thick and thin. Loyalty is one of the most cherished traits in a dog, and certain breeds have a remarkable ability to form deep, lifelong bonds with their owners. These dogs will always put their owners first. These dogs will always put their humans first, providing protection, emotional support, and unconditional love. If you're seeking a fury friend who will prove that loyalty truly is their superpower, these breeds are the perfect fit for you1. It is a small and delightful breed of dogs that has been a loyal companion since around the 16th century. Often seen in portrait paintings, the Papillion breed organized in France and was favorite dog of French royalty. Today, Papillion puppies for sale are in popular demand due to their affectionate nature and tiny size:

- Phalene dogs
- Continental Toy Spaniel
- Epagneul Nain Continental

These Papillion dogs have the following dimensions:

✓ Height

8-12 inches

✓ Weight

5-10 pounds

✓ Lifespan

14-16 years

✓ Breed group

Toy

✓ Shed level

✓ Temperament
Moderate

✓ Energy level
Friendly

✓ Common health concerns
Active

Dental disease, patellar luxation, open fontanelle

The Papillion dogs are European favorite with the following countries: France, Belgium, Spain, Italy, and the Netherlands. Beside these dogs, dachshund is popular in the United Kingdom, Germany (Their country of origin), and Australia.

Dog Insurance: They are a health insurance policy specifically designed to cover your *dog's medical needs.* The policies range from accident-only plans and accident-and-illness coverage to *wellness and lifetime* plans. Each type has its benefits and limitations, so that it's essential to *consider your dog's age, breed, and overall health,* as well as your budget when selecting *coverage for all the different dog breeds,* and the best pet insurance for dogs that allows the owners to customize the annual coverage limits, reimbursements percentages, and deductibles, ensuring the plan that meets their dog's specific needs.

❖ Spot Pet Insurance
❖ Pet's bets Health Insurance
❖ Embrace Pet Insurance
❖ Lemonade Pet Insurance

❖ Fetch Pet Insurance
❖ Pumpkin Multiple Pet Insurance
❖ Healthy Paws Chubb Company
❖ Chewy Care Plus Pet Insurance Company
❖ Prudent Pet Insurance
❖ Figo Pet Insurance Company
❖ Forbes Pet Insurance

Some dog breeds will attack children which include the following dogs:

1. *Pit Bull Terriers*

ates

Figure 39: Pit Bull (Adult) is an active large dog that can be aggressive and intimidating to many adults that are criminals, and the dog received the Hero Dog Award in 2025.

2. *German Shepherds:*

✓ Popular pets in the United States

✓ Often used by po... ...ites
✓ This is a commo... ...ild.

Figure: 41: Rottweilers (Adult) can be aggressive dogs, and they received the Hero Dog Award in 2024.

✓ ***Perro*** de ***Presa Canarios.*** They are considered one of the most dangerous dog breeds.

There are other dog breeds that cause dog bites on children that occur from dogs are familiar to the child. When pediatric facial dog bites occur to children between 5 and 9 years of age. Younger children are more prone to injuries to the face due to their smaller stature which is on the same level as the attacking dog. And will attack both male and female children. About 70% of the people were bitten by mixed breeds. Over 90% of the dogs were known to the patients; thus, the accuracy of the breed identification is expected to be high. What is clear from the data is that virtually any breed of dog can bite because of the related heredity, early experience, later socialization and training, health(Medical and behavioral), and victim behavior. The Pit Bulls in Denver, Colorado banned and the extreme injuries and the longest hospitalization of their entire population, indicating that despite legislation, the pit bull bites continue to be a public health concern.

The burden of the facial dog bite injuries is massive, from the financial costs to emotional and psychological tolls. The conservative annual estimates of the total cost of dog bite injuries range from $235 to 250 million. Of this, an estimated $62.5million is spent on hospital admissions. Much harder to calculate is the emotional distress victims and families that must deal with afterward. The number of unreported cases of emotional distress is likely higher than the reported and the need for early psychological support in victims is underestimated. Tantamount to this is providing education to parents, children, and the community. In addition, dogs need appropriate behavioral training. It is clear that children will most likely be the victims of a bite from a dog familiar to them, often their own dog. The impetus is on parents to recognize aggressive breeds as well as behaviors and never allow their young children to be left unsupervised around any dog. The weakness of the study is related to its retrospective nature and the fact that tracking and complete reporting of dog bites remains extremely problematic. Children 5 years old and younger are at high risk of being bitten in the face by a familiar dog and are more likely to require hospitalization than older children. The following dog causes many attack accidents:

- ➢ Akitas
- ➢ Cane Corsos
- ➢ Chihuahuas
- ➢ Chow Chows, Doberman Pinchers

California has the most dog bite incidents in the United States. California has the most dog bite claims, and more dogs than any other state because of the following:

1. *Dog bite incidents*: California has the most dog bite incidents in the United States, including the most dog bites on postal workers.

2. *Dog* bite *claims*: California has the most dog bite claims, with nearly 40% of the households owning at least one dog.

3. *Dog* bite *fatalities*: California and Texas have more fatal dog attacks than any other state.

4. *There are many states with many dog bites:*

   - ➢ *Texas*: Has many dog bite incidents, including fatal dog attacks.
   - ➢ *Florida:* Has many dog bite incidents, including fatal dog attacks.
   - ➢ *Ohio*: Has many dog bite incidents.

5. These are the states with dog attacks:

   - ➢ *California*

   2,104

   - ➢ *Florida*

➢ Texas

1,532

➢ Michigan

1,040

➢ Ohio

932

➢ Pennsylvania

885

➢ New York

857

➢ Illinois

851

$$837$$

➤ *New Jersey*

$$649$$

➤ *Georgia*

$$495$$

6. **The states with the least number of dog bites:**

✚ *Vermont*

$$35$$

✚ 4 *Wyoming*

$$34$$

✚ *South Dacota*

$$60$$

✚ *North Dakota*

$$50$$

✚ *Alaska*

$$52$$

Delaware

Montana

New Hampshire

125

120

Training your dogs can help save your dog from biting people. It is best that your puppy gets their mind in the correct place! This will help keep your dog with the least number of bites! Be sure to send the dog to a great trainer to behave better.

Figure 42: Perro de Presa Corarios dogs can be properly trained to prevent them from biting people if they are properly trained and received the Hero Dog Award in 2025.

The puppy's teeth and gum's health should be well taken care of, and they should brush the adult and senior dogs so they can be taken to a dog Vet to have them checked completely. Be sure to use a soft human toothbrush and a special dog

results:

Figure 43: Aitas dog has gone to the dentist on a regular basis to prevent the dog from biting children and receive the Hero Dog Award in 2025.

Figure 44: Care Corso's dog is a great dog that received the Hero Dog Award back in 1023.

Figure 45: Chihuahuas dog is a small dog, but can be very aggressive and bark a lot against the friendly community, but received the Hero Dog Award in 2025.

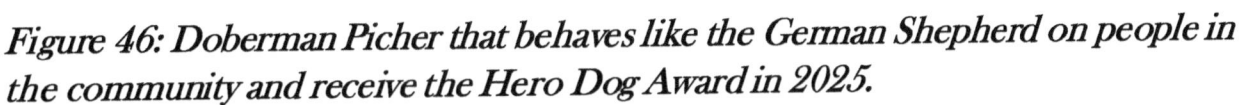

Figure 46: Doberman Picher that behaves like the German Shepherd on people in the community and receive the Hero Dog Award in 2025.

Chapter 9
Dog's Breeding Lessons

There is not a particular breed in America and in any event breeding dogs is a heartbreaking and backbreaking way to make a living. There are 13 states that breed dogs in the most popular way:

1. Alaska

Malamute

2. Georgia

French

Bulldog
3. Louisiana

Catahoula

Leopard
4. Maryland

Chesapeake

Bay Retriever
5. Massachusetts

Boston

Terrier
6. New Hampshire

Chinook

7. New York

Labrador
Retrievers
8. North Carolina

Australian

Shepherd
9. Pennsylvania

Great Dane

10. South Carolina

Boykin

Spaniel
11. Texas

Blue Lacy

12. Virginia

Foxhound

13. Wisconsin

American

Water Spaniel

Dogs breed when a male dog introduces sperm into a female's dog reproductive tract during her *estrus cycle*:

- ❖ *Proestrus*: The start of heat, when the female's vulva swells, and she bleeds. She attracts males but doesn't allow mounting.
- ❖ *Estrus*: The mating period, when the female's blood flow lessens and stops. She attracts and accepts males, and ovulation occurs.
- ❖ *Diestrus*: The period after heat, when the female is either pregnant or resting.
- ❖ *Anestrus*: The resting period between diestrus and the next cycle.

The mating process:

1. *Courtship*: The dogs sniff and lick each other's genital areas to gather scent and pheromones.
2. *Playful behaviors*: The female runs away and allows the male to catch her, and she flags her tail to signal readiness.
3. *Copulation*: The male introduces sperm into the female's reproductive tract.
4. *Tying:* The dogs may tie together tail-to-tail for a period of time.

Breeding preparation:

5. *Health checks*: Perform pre-breeding health checks on both dogs.
6. *Choose a mate*: Consider the dog's temperament, health, genetics, and pedigree.
7. *Finalize a contract*: Finalize a stud contract and set the stud fee.
8. *Tract heat cycles*: Tract the female's heat cycles to calculate when her next season is likely to be.

Figure 47. A dog rides safely in the owner's car

During breeding, the male dog mounts the female dog from the rear and clasps her midsection with his front legs. Rapid pelvic thrust follows until:

1. *Courtship*: The dogs sniff and lick each other's genital areas to gather scent and pheromones.

2. *Playful behaviors:* The female runs away and allows the male to catch her, and she flags her tail to signal readiness.
3. *Copulation:* The male introduces sperm into the female's reproductive tract.
4. *Tying:* The dogs may tie together tail-to-tail for a period of time.

Breeding preparation:

1. *Health checks:* Perform pre-breeding health checks on both dogs.
2. *Choose a mate:* Consider the dog's temperament, health, genetics, and pedigree.
3. *Finalize a contract:* Finalize a stud contract and set the stud fee.
4. *Tract heat cycles:* Tract the female's heat cycles to calculate when her next season is likely to be.

Figure 47. A dog rides safely in the owner's car after been properly trained by a professional trainer that received the Hero Dog Award in 2025.

During breeding, the male dog mounts the female dog from the rear and clasps her midsection with his front legs. Rapid pelvic thrust follows until penetration and ejaculation take place. Good puppies start long before mating ever takes place. Both parents need long-term pre-breeding care-what dog owners call conditioning-to produce the best offspring. This means regular veterinary care, screening for genetic problems, pre-breeding tests, and regular exercise and excellent nutrition. Bitches should not be overweight and should have good muscle tone before breeding. Additionally, a bitch that is in good mental condition that will make a better mother than a bitch that is insecure, snappy, or has an otherwise unstable temperament. One month before mating, the bitch should have a through pre-breeding physical examination by a veterinarian, and ideally a veterinarian who is well-versed in and supportive of canine reproduction. Her vaccinations should be in current condition and the dog should be tested and treated for parasites. You may also want to have the bitch and dog tested for brucellosis, an infectious bacterial disease that can cause sterility or spontaneous abortion in affected dogs. The age at which dogs reach sexual maturity depends to a large extent on their breed. Small breeds tend to mature faster than large breeds.

On average, however, males become fertile after six months of age and reach full sexual maturity by 12 to 15 months. Healthy stud dogs may remain sexually active and fertile to old age. Adult males are able to mate at any time. Bitches have their first estrus (Also known as "season" or "heat") after six months of age, although it can occur as late as 18 months to two years of age. Estrus recurs at intervals of approximately six months until late in life. During estrus, the female is fertile and will accept a male partner. The bitch should not be bred during her first season. The bitch's cycle is divided into four periods:

1. **Proestrus**: The bitch attracts males, has a bloody vaginal discharge, and her vulva is swollen. Proestrus lasts approximately 9 days: the bitch, however, will not allow breeding at this time.
2. **Estrus:** During this period, which also lasts approximately 9 days, the bitch will accept the male dog, and she is fertile. Ovulation usually occurs in the first 48 hours; however, this can vary greatly.
3. *Diestrus*: Lasting 60 to 90 days, diestrus is the period when the reproductive track is under the control of the hormone progesterone. This occurs whether or not the bitch becomes pregnant. False pregnancy, a condition in which the bitch shows symptoms of being pregnant although she has not conceived, is occasionally seen during diestrus.
4. Anestrus: No sexual activity takes place. Anestrus lasts between 3 and 4months. Keep in mind that AKC rules do not allow, except with special documentation, the registration of a litter out of a dam less than 8months of age or more than 12 years of age at the time of mating.

Making natural breeding:

Responsible dog breeders generally do not breed a breed a bitch at the first heat to avoid imposing the stress of pregnancy and lactation on a young, growing animal. It is also customary to avoid breeding a bitch on consecutive heats to allow sufficient time for recuperation between pregnancies. Most dogs are first bred between the 10th and 14th day after the onset of proestrus. As long as the bitch will accept the male dog, mating every other day for a total of two or three matings is generally considered sufficient. However, signs of proestrus are not obvious in some bitches. To catch the peak fertile period, a veterinarian may need to perform hormone tests or examine vaginal smears under a microscope. The bitches are usually less inhibited by new environments so that they are usually taken to the stud. Breeding involving young males proceed more smoothly if they are paired with experienced bitches. Sometimes human handlers must step in with assistance or guidance during bleedings. Some breeds are more prone to needing assistance than others because of anatomical considerations. Discussing this process with your own breeder will help you to be prepared for how you may need to assist. During breeding, the male dog mounts the female dog from the rear and clasps her midsection with his front legs. Rapid pelvic thrust follows until penetration and ejaculation take place. After the pelvic thrust case, the dog and bitch will not separate the dogs during the tie because it can injure either or both animals. After some time, they will part naturally.

Artificial Insemination:

This procedure is a relatively simple procedure that can be used when natural breeding is impractical. The AKC accepts registration of a litter mated by artificial insemination using fresh semen, fresh extended semen, and frozen semen, provided the proper procedures that are followed. Registration of these letters requires DNA certification. For more information, see the AKC's rules for registering a litter bred by artificial insemination.

Pregnancy and Whelping Preparation Watch for Signs of Pregnancy:

Canine gestation lasts approximately 63 days. Signs of pregnancy include an increase in appetite, weight, and nipple size. However, a bitch with false pregnancy may also show these signs. The veterinarian can usually confirm a pregnancy through abdominal palpitation at 28 days, or by using ultrasound or X-rays. Once pregnancy is confirmed, you should talk to your vet about special feeding requirements and what to expect during pregnancy, labor, and after birth. You should also be briefed on how to recognize and respond to an emergency.

Provide Proper Nutrition for Your Pregnant Bitch:

A bitch in good condition should continue into pregnancy with the same caloric intake that the dog had during the adult maintenance. The dog food intake should be increased only as their body weight increases, beginning about the last five weeks before whelping. Daily food intake should be increased gradually, so that at the time of whelping the female dog may be eating 35 to 50 percent more than usual. As their weight and food intake increase, they begin offering small, frequent meals to spare them the discomfort that larger meals can cause, especially in a small dog. If you have been feeding your bitch a well-balanced, high-quality diet, you should not need to add anything to their food during their pregnancy. However, some breeders advocate supplementation with a protein source such as evaporated milk, eggs, meat, or liver. These supplements should never represent more than 10% of the bitch's daily food intake.

Accustom Your Bitch to the Whelping Box:

It is a good idea to build a whelping box well in advanced, so the bitch has time to become accustomed to it. Unless you are already accustomed to it. Unless you are already accustomed to a whelping box, she may choose your closest or another inappropriate place for a delivery room. An ideal whelping environment is warm, dry, quiet, draft-free, and away from all other dogs when possible. Confinement and whelping location of your bitch is relative to her breed and size. A good whelping box is roomy and has low sides so you can easily reach it. It should also have a small shelf or roll bars running halfway up along the sides, so the pups have something to crawl under to avoid getting rolled on by the bitch. Many breeders prefer to line the box with newspapers until after delivery because paper can be changed quickly when it becomes soiled. After whelping newspapers are typically replaced with non-skid bathmats, outdoor carpeting, or something else that provides better footing for the puppies.

Be Alert for Signs of Labor:

A few days before the bitch is ready to give birth, she may stop eating and start building a "nest" where she plans to have her puppies. If it was introduced properly, this should be in the whelping box that you have prepared for her. Shortly before whelping, the bitch's body temperature will drop to 99 degrees or lower (From a normal temperature of 100 to 102.5degrees). Approximately 24 hours after her temperature drops, she can be expected to enter the first stage of labor when the cervix dilates and opens the birth canal for the passage of puppies. At this time, she will pant, strain, and appear restless. This stage of labor is followed by actual abdominal straining and production of the puppies and placentas. You should have on hand your veterinarian's phone number and the number for your local emergency veterinary clinic.

Puppies are born:

Most bitches gave birth easily without the need of human help. Each puppy emerges in its own placental membrane, or sac, which must be removed before the puppy can breathe. The mother usually takes care of this by tearing off (And sometimes eating) the membrane and then servers the umbilical cord. After delivery, she will lick each puppy to stimulate its breathing. You should keep track of how many placentas are delivered and ensured that the number matches the number puppies, because a retained placenta may cause problems for the bitch. You must take over if the bitch neglects to remove a sac or sever an umbilical cord. A puppy can remain inside the sac for only a few minutes before the oxygen supply is depleted. The sac membrane should be torn near the puppy's head and peeled backward until the puppy can be gently removed. Then you should clear away mucus or fluids from the puppy's mouth and nose and gently rub the puppy with a towel to stimulate circulation. The umbilical cord can be tied with unwaxed dental floss and cut on the far side of the tie/knot about two inches from the abdomen. The cut end should be painted with iodine to prevent infection.

At time of birth, the bitch will be busy cleaning her puppies, warming them, and allowing them to suckle. It is very important for the puppies to suckle soon after emerging from the womb. Suckling lets them ingest colostrum, a milk-like substance containing maternal antibodies which is produced in the mammary glands just after birth. Colostrum helps the newborn puppies fight infection in their early days while their own immune systems mature. To track nourishment of the puppies, it is advisable to identify and weigh the puppies during the first 2 weeks.

Consult Your Veterinarian If Complications Arise:

If something goes wrong, don't hesitate to call your veterinarian or emergency clinic for assistance. The signs of potential trouble include:

➢ Indications of extreme pain
➢ Strong contractions lasting for more than 45 minutes without delivery of a pup
➢ More than two hours elapsing between puppies with or without delivery of a pup
➢ More than 2 hours elapsing between puppies with or without contractions
➢ Trembling, shivering, or collapse of the dogs
➢ Passing a dark green or bloody fluid before the birth of the first puppy (After the first puppy, this is normal)
➢ No signs of labor by the 6th day after her last mating

Keep your puppies warm, fed and clean:

A newborn puppy cannot control its body temperature and must be kept in a warm environment. Chilling will stress the puppy and predispose it to infectious disease; overheating can kill it. The environmental temperature can be controlled with a well-insulated electric heating pad or a heat lamp; but make sure that the puppies have a cooler place to crawl to if they become too warm. The immediate environmental temperature should be kept between 85 and 90 degrees for the first five days of life.

So, you have decided to get a new puppy. Whether this is a first-time pet or an addition to the family, there are several things that you need to get ahead of time and there's some planning to do. There are whole books written on this subject, so this will by no means be an exhaustive list but will include the most important points to consider.

Establish a veterinary relationship early:

Before bringing your puppy home, decide on a veterinary clinic or hospital to care for your puppy's health. Even if you currently have a veterinarian for your other pets, ask when you should have your new puppy examined. Most veterinarians recommended an exam within 3 to 5 days of getting your new puppy evaluated any health issues. At the first appointment, the vet will work with you to establish a vaccination and parasite control plan to keep your puppy healthy and free of illness.

Dog food:

The puppies have specific nutritional requirements to support their growth and development, *Loyall Life Puppy and Loyall Life Puppy Large Breed* contains a balance of essential nutrients to support the all-important start to a healthy life.

Food and water bowls:

Puppies need to eat three times a day, so the food bowls work the best and harbor less bacteria than plastic or glass. Additionally, with a wider base will provide additional the puppies are not delicate eaters, so a food and water bowl with a wider base will provide additional stability.

Collar or Harness:

Buy an appropriately sized, adjustable collar or harness making sure that they wear it regularly. The collar or harness should be tight enough to fit two fingers between it and your puppy. Remember to check it weekly as your puppy grows and buy a new, larger one as needed.

Leash:

Puppies are not born knowing how to walk on a leash. This is an important socialization skill that they must learn. The leash should be 4 to 6 feet long and allow you to walk comfortably with your puppy while still maintaining control.

Create or Carrier:

Dogs are den animals. They find comfort and security in an enclosed, intimate space that they can adapt as their own. Choose a crate or carrier your dog can grow into and move around in but not so big that they can eliminate in one corner and sleep in another.

Grooming:

Depending on your dog's coat, you'll need a comb, brush or shedding blade. Routine brushing will keep your puppy's hair coat clean and shiny and also help you create a bond with your new puppy.

Bathing Supplies:

At some point, your puppy will need a bath! You'll need pet shampoo, cotton balls for the ears, a sterile eye ointment, and towels and sponge.

Cleaning products:

Even the most well-behaved puppy will have an accident in the house. Having natural cleaning products on hand will help with the safe cleanup of accidents. Consider using an enzyme-based cleaning product since these will break down pet odors rather than just masking them.

Puppy pads and newspapers:

Waterproof puppy pads can be useful under bedding in the crate to aid in cleaning up and help protect the floor but should not be used as a potty-training tool in the house. Using puppy pads and newspapers are potty-training tools that only give your puppy permission to eliminate in the house behavior you probably want to avoid.

Chew toys: Puppies will chew anything in their path. It is natural exploration behavior, but one that can be hazardous to your shoes, clothing and household stuff. Choose a variety of age and size appropriate toys.

Key points to remember:

Warmth:

- ➢ Newborn puppies can't regulate their body temperature, so provide a warm environment with a heat lamp or monitor their comfort level and adjust heating pad in their whelping box, keeping the temperature around 85-90 degrees during the first few days during winter.
- ➢ Monitor their control level and adjust the temperature as needed.
- ➢ If separated from their mother, consider puppy sweaters or jackets to maintain warmth.

Feeding:

- ❖ Supply a machine with material, power, or other things necessary for the operation.
- ❖ Supply water (A body of water), the pond is fed by a small stream.
- ❖ Insert further coins into a meter to extend the time for which it expires.
- ❖ Supply someone with information, ideas, and readings.
- ❖ Prompt an actor with a line; you may be still in the wings feeding the dogs some food.

- Cause to move gradually and steadily, typically through a confined space to make holes through which to feed the cables.
- Influence or contribute to feed into the artwork.
- The act or process of eating or being fed
- Exclusive breast milk feeding rates, birth-friendly practices and reporting on racial/ethnic disparities.
- Many female dogs act properly for their 3 to 9 puppies being fed properly while they are blind for 2 to 3 weeks.

Chapter 10
Dog's Clothing Lessons

The dog's sweater may help your dog to be warm during the winter weather. Sweaters are one comfortable dog's warming clothing. Be careful to measure your dog to achieve a proper fit for your dog. Be sure to obtain your dog's clothing to fit properly so that when the urinates or contemplates to poop, be sure that the clothing does not interfere with your dog's attempts. Many sweaters fit the dog's two front legs and front body. There is the following example:

➢ Large

(14-20 pounds]

➢ Neck size

12.5 inches

➢ Chest size

19 inches

➢ Minimum weight

14 pounds

➢ Here are other considerations that are important:

- **_Stretchy and Comfy_**: This pullover dog sweater is stretchy and allows for full dog's movement without restricting the shoulders. It can stretch easily in all sides to fit the diverse body shape of the pets. Wearing it all day, the fleece jacket provides the utmost comfy.
- **_Reflective Dog Sweatshirt_**: Pay attention to the type of material, the color, and purpose of the clothing. Many clothing is worn in the hospital or for wearing with the dog's owner.

- ***Reporting:*** The dog should have writings to inform people in the hospital or outside that it is informative what people should know.
- ***Informative:*** The dog should be smart and report their information to the public audience.

Chapter 11
Dog's Diet and Foods

The salmon protein helps avoid a dog's reaction to food. The company, Purina, makes dog foods that are sensitive to the dog's skin and stomach which is a dry formula. Their Pro Plan is good digestive health, bone health, and sensitive to your dog's skin, stomach, muscle. Chicken and Brown Rice Dog Food is a very popular brand of dog food. The other famous dog foods are the following:

- ❖ Dr. Pol Incredi-Pol Beef & Brown Rice Dog Food
- ❖ Dr. Pol Salmon Recipe Dry Dog Food
- ❖ Dr. Pol Chicken Recipe Dog Food
- ❖ Purina One Dry Dog Food
- ❖ Pet's Table developed with vet nutritionists
- ❖ Ollie are human-grade food made from real ingredients
- ❖ Spot & Tango with USDA human-grade meats
- ❖ We Feed Raw Pet Food Company have dog foods designed for Dog's biology
- ❖ Nom Nom has dog food formulated by veterinary nutritionists
- ❖ Blue Life Protection Formula for dogs
- ❖ Fresh Pet Custom Meals for dogs
- ❖ Just Food for Dogs
- ❖ Open Farm Grass-fed Beef
- ❖ Pedigree Complete Nutrition Adult Dry Dog Food
- ❖ Just Food for Dogs Sampler Variety Frozen Human-Grade Fresh Dog Food
- ❖ Dr. Marty Nature's Blend Essential Wellness Freeze-Dried Raw Dog Food
- ❖ ACANA Butcher's Favorite Dry Dog Food
- ❖ FRESH pet Select Dog Food Tender Chicken Recipe
- ❖ Open Farm Ancient Grains Homestead Turkey Dry Dog Food
- ❖ Mini Chunk Savory Chicken Flavor Dry Dog Food
- ❖ Stella & Chewy's Wild Red Dry Dog Food
- ❖ Sundays for Dogs all-natural Chicken Dog Food
- ❖ Taste of the Wild Dog Food
- ❖ Purina Beyond Dog Foods
- ❖ Gentle Giants All Life Stages Natural Non-GMO Beef and Bacon Dry Dog Food
- ❖ Chewy's Chicken Meal Mixers

Figure 48. Puppies are a handful to keep them happy and active with the children and have the professional dog trainer that has the Hero Dog Award.

The dog's heart worms must be removed by an animal vet so that the dog can get well soon.

About 4 million dogs owned by American Dog owners have their dogs euthanized by private dog companies and be very sad about this poor happing's!
My favorite behavior of my senior dogs is their behavior of sleeping during the night and part of the day!

Figure 49: A house cat sleeping on the owner's big fluffy dog and the Hero Dog Award was provided to the indoor dog.

Friendly house cats try to find a friendly dog to sleep on at night or even during the day! I listed the dogs that will participate in the house cats sleeping with an older dog. The owners will be so proud of their older dogs!

Chapter 12
Dog's Playful Toys

There is interactive dog toys with motion activated, squeaky dog toy active rolling ball Wicked Ball for daily dogs. The Devil Dog Pet Company sells the Himalayan Yak Chews, Yak Cheese Dog Chews that are 100% natural and Healthy. There is a 2025 upgrade Smart Interactive Dog Toys which are Wicked Ball Air; there are Interactive Modes:

❖ Self-Moving Bouncing Rotating Ball of E-TPU material and IPX7 waterproof
❖ Active Rolling Ball for Medium and Large dogs.

To match your dog's play style and energy level. This dog toy offers mental stimulation and endless fun, perfect for keeping your dog happy and entertained. The material of the round ball is thermoplastic polyurethane. You can buy the following:

➤ Dog chest commuter strap	$25
➤ Pet automatic feeder	$190
➤ Automatic retractable pet leash	$30
➤ Pet nail polisher and clipper	$25
➤ Portable dog kettle	$20
➤ Tumbler balance dog training toy	$25
➤ Tactical dog harness	$40
➤ Dog pooper scooper built-in poop bag dispenser	$20
➤ Vacuum cleaner for dogs	$120
➤ Silicone food tray for dog	$25
➤ Adjustable pet leash for jogging	$18
➤ Smell dog bed	$647
➤ Freebie for you and your dog to play with by watching a video that your dog can watch to be excellent player	$3-5

What stores can you go to:

✓ Tractor Supply Company	330-792-8235
✓ Pet Supplies Plus	330-886-8986
✓ Pets Are People Too	330-565-0583
✓ Petland	412-499-3536
✓ Harbor Pet Center	330-846-1982

My favorite behavior of my senior dogs is their behavior of sleeping!

Figure 49: A house cat sleeping on the owner's big fluffy dog.

Friendly house cats try to find a friendly dog to sleep on at night or even during the day! I listed the dogs that will participate in the house cats sleeping with an older dog. The owners will be so proud of their older dogs!

Figure 50:   My favorite and outstanding barber who cuts my hair at *"Heidi's Hair Salon"* at 4269 224 Avenue in Boardman, Ohio 45631, is when Ms. Perry will trim my hair to look good and she trims, shapes and uses a dye for my wife's hair in an outstanding fashion to keep her looking young and attractive. The shop's telephone number is 330-719-6808. A hard-working Ms. Perry goes home to relax and sometimes sleep with her puppy that she loves, like her real baby. She greatly loves her puppy named *Bean,* to lay around at 6:00P.M. for about an hour. This is a remarkable photograph of her and her lovely puppy that rest together